Your Towns and Cities in

Pontefract and Castleford
in the Great War

Your Towns and Cities in the Great War

Pontefract and Castleford in the Great War

Tim Lynch

Pen & Sword
MILITARY

First published in Great Britain in 2016 by
PEN & SWORD MILITARY
an imprint of
Pen and Sword Books Ltd
47 Church Street
Barnsley
South Yorkshire S70 2AS

Copyright © Tim Lynch, 2016

ISBN 978 1 47385 215 0

The right of Tim Lynch to be identified as the author of
this work has been asserted by him in accordance with the Copyright,
Designs and Patents Act 1988.

A CIP record for this book is available from the British Library

Printed and bound in England
by CPI Group (UK) Ltd, Croydon, CR0 4YY

Typeset in Times New Roman by Chic Graphics

Pen & Sword Books Ltd incorporates the imprints of
Pen & Sword Archaeology, Atlas, Aviation, Battleground, Discovery,
Family History, History, Maritime, Military, Naval, Politics, Railways,
Select, Social History, Transport, True Crime, Claymore Press,
Frontline Books, Leo Cooper, Praetorian Press, Remember When,
Seaforth Publishing and Wharncliffe.

For a complete list of Pen and Sword titles please contact
Pen and Sword Books Limited
47 Church Street, Barnsley, South Yorkshire, S70 2AS, England
E-mail: enquiries@pen-and-sword.co.uk
Website: www.pen-and-sword.co.uk

Contents

Acknowledgements

I would like to dedicate this book to my father, Albert Lynch, a child of the generation that lived through the Great War. It was on family holidays to Belgium and France and childhood visits to the battlefields of Waterloo, Ypres and Dunkirk that my love of history was born.

Thanks go to Roni Wilkinson at Pen & Sword for the opportunity to write about Pontefract and Castleford – both towns I know well having worked in each – and for the excuse to go rummaging around in archives. I know that makes me an anorak but at least it's indoors and doesn't involve heavy lifting so has to be better than a proper job.

As ever, special thanks to my family, Jacqui, Beth and Josh, for their patience and ability to demonstrate a remarkable range of interest in the obscure facts I bring to the dinner table after a day spent reading old newspapers.

Efforts have been made to establish the copyright ownership of the images used. No harm or injury is intended by their use and if information is forthcoming, appropriate credit will be included in any future editions.

Introduction

Castleford, Ferrybridge, Ferry Fryston, Wentbridge – names that speak of the importance in years gone by of the crossings over the River Aire to traffic heading up and down the Great North Road. Even the name Pontefract translates as 'broken bridge'. The town's fame may be based on coal and liquorice, but for millennia Pontefract has stood as a crucial waystation on Britain's fatal avenue.

A Roman settlement guarded the crossing at Castleford that enabled Legionaries to ford the river on their way to their northern outposts. According to the Anglo-Saxon Chronicle, in the year 947 Eadred, 'King of the English', came to Tanshelf, where Wulfstan, Archbishop of York, and all the councillors of the Northumbrians pledged themselves to him. Soon afterwards they betrayed their oaths and instead took the Viking Erik Bloodaxe as their king. In response, the following year Eadred attacked Northumbria and burnt down St Wilfrid's minster at Ripon, but as Eadred's army made their way home, a Viking army from York caught up with him at Castleford and the battle claimed a great many lives. This so enraged Eadred that he threatened to march back into Northumbria and destroy it utterly, at which point the Northumbrians deserted Erik and paid Eadred compensation.

The Norman invasion of 1066 saw Pontefract established as a base for the harrying of the north as Ilbert de Lacy established a fortress on land granted to him by William the Conqueror, with power over lands from Hull to the Pennines. For a time the castle belonged to King John and the original Robin Hood stories place him at Barnsdale Bar, just outside the town, fighting a guerrilla war against the corrupt aristocracy. In 1322, Thomas, Earl of Lancaster, was sentenced to death in the castle's great hall and beheaded outside the walls. Richard II is believed to have been murdered in the castle and troops marching towards the killing fields of Towton in 1461 camped on the grounds outside before the battle. By the time of the civil war, Cromwell regarded Pontefract as 'one of the strongest inland garrisons in the kingdom', suffering no fewer than three sieges until the locals, fed up of the castle's ability to attract trouble, petitioned for it to be 'slighted'. In 1649, demolition work began.

The area settled down into a period of peace and prosperity. The local soil proved ideal for the cultivation of liquorice and, in the early 1800s, 'Pontefract Cakes' began to appear in sweetshops across the country. The Industrial Revolution brought with it an almost insatiable demand for the coal that lay beneath the surface in a seam running through Doncaster and Selby via Pontefract and Castleford. Industry brought rapid growth – Castleford's population in 1801 was given as just 1,587 people but by the outbreak of the Great War it had risen to 23,090. Such growth placed pressure on housing and sanitation so much, that by the mid-1890s, one in five babies died before their first birthday, often of diseases like diarrhoea carried by flies from stinking middens shared by up to twenty households. Pollution blocked out the sun for days on end and caused breathing problems in young and old.

In 1893, around 250,000 miners nationwide demanded what they termed 'a living wage' at a time when pit owners responded to a fall in coal prices by cutting wages to protect profits. At Featherstone's two pits, Lord Masham decided to lock out his workers until they agreed to a reduction in wages, knowing they would soon be starved into submission. On 5 September, riots began in pit villages in Derbyshire and protests spread across the country. The Featherstone miners gathered around men loading coal to supply the vast Lister's Mill in Bradford – part of Lord Masham's business empire. Angry at what they considered a betrayal of their loyalty and that Lord Masham was profiting while they went hungry, the miners and their families blamed the pit manager, Alfred Holiday, who was assisting in the movement of coal. Holiday claimed this was for the pit engines rather than the Bradford mill, but no one believed him and a group of strikers attacked the men loading the coal. Panicked, Holiday rushed to the local Pontefract police for assistance, but they were sympathetic to the strikers and sent him to Wakefield where by chance he met Lord St Oswald, another local pit owner, who was there seeking protection for his own mine. Wakefield police decided that troops should be brought in and that afternoon, twenty-nine soldiers of the 1st Battalion South Staffordshire Regiment, under the command of Captain Barker, arrived to face a growing crowd of angry miners and onlookers. A later report claimed that some of the mob threw stones and others set fires that could be seen 'for miles round'. Hundreds more spectators appeared, many from outside Featherstone.

That evening, local magistrate Bernard Hartley JP read the Riot Act, ordering the crowd to disperse and warning that those remaining after one hour had passed could be arrested. What happened next remains unclear. An anonymous tract published soon afterwards by the *Anarchist Journal* described the scene as relatively peaceful. Local police saw no cause for concern until a group of strangers arrived in town armed with cudgels and threatened to kill Holiday, whipping the crowd into a frenzy.

The soldiers had by then established themselves in a room on the first floor of the engine house and suddenly found themselves under attack. 'A storm of stones and pieces of iron came crashing into the room', and Captain Barker looked out to see 'a swarm of men and boys armed with sticks and bludgeons' closing in. Fires were started and the situation was turning very nasty. Barker called on the strikers to allow his men to withdraw and the soldiers were allowed to leave the pit, surrounded by a jeering crowd as they made their way to the railway station. There they regrouped and watched the pit burn until ordered back in by the magistrate. A fire engine from Pontefract had been attacked as it tried to reach the fire and Hartley demanded the soldiers do something to restore order. Barker told his men to fix bayonets and they cleared a path through the mob.

Faced with armed soldiers, a report claimed someone shouted that 'we would rather be shot than hungered to death', and the crowd closed in again. Some thought the soldiers had first fired blanks as a warning shot that failed, others claimed they deliberately aimed low with live ammunition. Whatever the truth, the second volley injured eight people, two fatally. It was later said that neither of the two dead men had been protesting, although what they were doing was never established. In any case, a Wakefield inquest concluded that the death of one was 'justifiable homicide'. The inquest into the other death took place in Featherstone itself where the jury blamed the lack of police and Holiday's overreaction. The different verdicts led to a parliamentary commission being set-up that eventually awarded £100 compensation to the families of the two dead men but nothing to the injured. The Secretary of State, Herbert Asquith, saw popular support fall as his nickname 'The Featherstone Murderer' spread among the working classes. Such incidents were becoming commonplace as workers fought for their livelihoods and relations between the military and civilians across the north would remain strained right up until 1914, trade unions even advising their members against joining the territorial force in case they were called upon to shoot down their colleagues and friends.

Many of the generation who went to war in 1914, then, had no love for the military. Their lives were bound up in a constant struggle for simple survival. Yet they believed in their country. They did not question the right of those in power to command, only the way in which they exercised that command. The kaiser had openly supported the Boers in South Africa against British rule and, ever since, people had been bombarded with anti-German propaganda in books, plays and at displays and festivals. In 1906, William Le Queux's novel *The Invasion of 1910* had been a global bestseller, describing a German landing in nearby Goole and the ensuing enslavement of first the industrial West Riding and then the whole of Britain. In 1914, the people of Britain fought not for ideals of king and country, but because they believed they were fighting to defend their very homes. What happened over the next four years would take over every aspect of their daily lives and change their world forever.

This is the story of how those events were felt by the communities around Pontefract.

A tract published in Sheffield by the Anarchist Journal *to report on the 'Featherstone Massacre'.*

BULLETS for BREAD!

✳ ✳ ✳

THE

FEATHERSTONE

MASSACRE.

WE WOULD RATHER BE SHOT DOWN THAN HUNGERED TO DEATH.

One Penny.

Working in harsh conditions from childhood meant that miners were able to cope well with the rigours of military service.

CHAPTER 1

'The lamps are going out all over Europe...'

At 10.45am on 28 June 1914, the Austrian Archduke Franz Ferdinand and his wife Sophie left the Town Hall in Sarajevo in a motorcade heading for the city's hospital. Earlier that morning two Serbian nationalists posted on the route into the city as part of an assassination plot had decided at the last moment not to go through with their plan but a third man, standing nearby, had thrown a bomb at Ferdinand's borrowed Graf and Stift convertible. The device skidded across the car's roof and fell into the road, exploding as the following vehicle drove over it and wounding at least sixteen bystanders. After reading a speech at the Town Hall as planned, his notes spattered with the blood of a wounded aide, Ferdinand asked to change the planned itinerary and go to visit the injured in hospital. Mistaken orders to the driver took the car down a wrong turning and directly into the path of 19-year-old Gavrilo Princip, another member of the Serbian group conspiring to kill Ferdinand. Princip was so hemmed in by the crowd that he was unable to pull out and prime the bomb he was carrying so instead he reached for his pistol, but couldn't move enough to actually aim it. According to his own testimony, Princip confessed, 'Where I aimed I do not know,' adding that he had raised his gun 'against the automobile without aiming. I even turned my head as I shot.' The killer fired just two bullets but one hit Sophie in the stomach while the other

Police arrest a member of the gang of Serbs who set out to assassinate Franz Ferdinand, June 1914.

hit the heir to the throne in the neck, severing his jugular vein. There was nothing any doctor could have done to save either of them. Both victims remained seated upright while being driven to the governor's residence for medical treatment. As reported by Count Harrach, Franz Ferdinand's last words were 'Sophie, Sophie! Don't die! Live for our children!' Sophie was dead on arrival at the governor's residence. Franz Ferdinand died ten minutes later.

The murders shocked the diplomatic world, but the deaths of an obscure archduke and his wife in a country far away meant little to the majority of people in Britain, whose main concerns were the weather, continuing strikes and a spate of attacks by militant suffragettes. A heatwave was gripping the nation with temperatures hitting 90 degrees in the shade in London and ten people had been reported as dying as a result of heatstroke. The news from Sarajevo was overshadowed by the events of the afternoon of Wednesday, 1 July when, almost as a portent of things to come, the heatwave ended with a devastating thunderstorm that exploded over Britain. 'The lightning was unusually vivid and almost continuous,' reported the *Yorkshire Post*, 'and the thunderclaps came like a series of sharp explosions.' Bradford city centre was flooded, as were parts of Leeds. At Carlton, 17-year-old Ernest Rhodes was struck by lightning as he led his horses across the railway near his home and had to be carried indoors. Nearby, a month-old baby was found with injuries to her arms and face. 'There is little hope the baby will recover,' reported the papers. At Castleford, 5 yards of tiles were knocked off the Allerton Stores and, at Potwell Farm near Pontefract, James Booth went to warn his neighbour, farmer Henry Harrison, that one of his stacks was ablaze. Harrison was found nearby, apparently killed by the same bolt that had started the fire.

As news of storm-damage filtered in over the next few days, one story featured widely, even being reported in the national press. When the storm broke, 29-year-old Isaac Barnes of Albion Street, Castleford, had been sitting on the doorstep of 8 Wood Street when lightning

Militant suffragettes were responsible for a wave of bombings across Britain as part of their campaign.

Marketplace, Pontefract c1914.

struck. According to reports at the time, Barnes was 'deprived of the use of his legs' and cried out 'Mother! I'm blind!' Friends carried him home and put him to bed 'feeling sore all over'. Two days later, newspapers as far afield as Dundee and South Glamorgan carried the story of how, as a second storm began, Barnes fell out of bed and found his sight miraculously restored.

Later that month, the local news was dominated by the visit of Princess Marie Louise to open a bazaar in Castleford to raise funds for new church buildings. One local dignitary told the crowd that he was not quite sure that: 'if I had had the privilege of examining Her Highness in geography, say twelve months ago, whether she would have been able to say where Castleford was. Of course, as soon as she knew that there was such an important place, she accepted the invitation to come there.' The event was hailed as a great success.

At the end of the month the great and the good again descended on the area to celebrate the 21st birthday of Rowland George Winn, eldest son of Lord St Oswald, at Nostell Priory. Rowland's birthday on

Carlton Street c1915. It was along here that some of the most violent anti-German rioting took place.

Wednesday, 29 July marked the start of four days of celebrations as men and officials of Frodingham Ironstone Mines presented him with 'an illuminated address' – a finely carved oak casket contained a book illustrated with drawings linked to his family and life including pictures of men at work in the family's mines and scenes from around their estates and holdings in Lincolnshire. Members of the Lincolnshire Iron Master's Association, along with tradespeople from Wakefield and Pontefract and tenants and employees of the Nostell estate, were all treated to lunch in the grounds. The next day, 1,300 employees of Nostell Colliery were invited for tea and, on Friday, another 1,300 employees of the family's Lincolnshire estate were brought by special trains for another celebratory tea. Saturday was reserved for special guests to celebrate not only Rowland's majority, but also Lord St Oswald's own 58th birthday. Proposing a toast, Jonathan Shaw explained how he had known the whole family since the present lord's grandfather and found them all to be true gentlemen. 'Surely with such examples before him the young gentleman … ought not to go astray.' A year later, though, some began to wonder if he had.

As thousands of ordinary people enjoyed Nostell's hospitality, events in Europe had already spiralled out of control. Austria, supported by Germany, blamed Serbia for the killing of the heir to the Austro-Hungarian Empire. The Serbian government, backed by Russia, denied involvement. Throughout July, the dispute escalated until, in order to support their respective allies, Germany and Russia mobilised their armies. At the end of the month Russia offered to negotiate a demobilisation, but by then it was too late. On 1 August, Germany declared war. France, tied to Russia by a mutual protection alliance, was forced to begin to mobilise its forces before Germany could execute its longstanding plan to invade France via neutral Belgium. Germany, they believed, would try to knock France out of the war as quickly as possible so they could turn their main effort on Russia.

On 2 August, Germany invaded Luxemburg and on the following day formally declared war on France. On 4 August, claiming to be

Rowland Winn, son of Lord St Oswald, owner of Nostell Priory, as a cadet prior to joining the Guards. Rowland's 21st birthday was marked by days of celebrations during which thousands of employees were brought to parties in the grounds.

*Crowds gather outside Buckingham Palace soon after the declaration of war,
August 1914.*

responding to a French attack, the Germans invaded Belgium. Having been one of the guarantors of Belgian neutrality, Britain was now forced to act. With a massive overseas empire, Britain could not allow international law to be flouted, nor could it allow Germany, the only naval power in the world able to challenge the Royal Navy, to establish itself in the English Channel where, once France was defeated, there would be no barrier to an invasion of England. Conflict was now inevitable and at 11pm on 4 August, Britain declared war on Germany.

Across the country, the August bank holiday was extended as people struggled to come to terms with what had happened. After years of anti-German propaganda, some welcomed the news, while others were still pleading through the newspapers and public meetings for every effort to be made to negotiate peace as quickly as possible and argued that this was a European matter Britain should not be drawn into. Glasshoughton pit remained closed because of a shortage of wagons, but even if they had been available, much of its production was exported and stocks had nowhere to go. Uncertain of their status and conscious of the insurance risks of putting to sea in wartime, ships remained in port. The railway networks were ordered to prioritise military transport and trade everywhere very quickly ground to an almost complete stop. No one knew what was likely to happen to the economy. Banks closed to prevent customers withdrawing their savings and new paper bank notes were released to try to safeguard the country's gold reserves. In Halifax, an emergency meeting of the Homing Society met and agreed to end the homing pigeon racing season early to avoid the risk of their members being arrested for spying.

The main worry for everyone, though, was food. Prices soared as shops faced an unprecedented demand. 'Closed doors – ', reported the *Pontefract Express* at the end of the first week of war:

> *That has been the order with the leading Pontefract grocers during some part of the week – chiefly for the whole of Wednesday afternoon. The reason was that they were unable to cope with the rush of orders sent in by those who had been seized with panic as to the price of foodstuffs – flour, sugar etc. It is to*

be hoped by this time the words of the Chancellor of the Exchequer, of the Prime Minister, of the Mayor of Pontefract and others have been properly appreciated by those who have given tradesmen a needlessly strenuous time during the week. The more rush there is for foodstuffs at this stage the higher will prices be forced up. We had an interview yesterday with Mr Geo. Hemmant yesterday and he spoke ... very strongly of the very poor and unpatriotic spirit which some of the public of Pontefract are showing by madly rushing for foods and thereby putting their poorer neighbours at great disadvantage. This attitude of "No1 first" shows very badly, says Mr Hemmant, at a time when thousands are prepared to sacrifice their lives, if need be, for their country.

In Castleford, where one store reported stocks enough to last six weeks, many shops restricted service to regular customers only and limited the amounts that could be purchased. So great was the problem across the country that the government had to arrange the compulsory purchase of all essentials so that prices could be controlled.

A dramatic 'dash for liberty' by Ms Irene Waller and her students also made the paper that week. The granddaughter of a local magistrate, Ms Waller had been at a graduation ceremony at the convent school in Heusdan on Sunday when a telegram arrived to announce that the last boat for England would leave the following morning. With the young people in her care 'properly chaperoned', as the paper hurried to assure its readers, the group hurriedly left on a five-hour journey to the port of Antwerp, where they watched in horror as armed guards prevented a group of men attempting to board the ship. After a ten-hour wait, the ship sailed so full that it meant 'even some young girls having to sleep on open deck'. Similar tales drifted in over the coming weeks of local people who had been in Europe when war broke out and their adventures in getting home. Former King's School teacher Percy Gould told of his escape from Paris aboard an overcrowded train, and C.P. Finn, manager of the Coke Ovens and By Product Plant for South Kirby, Featherstone and Hemsworth Collieries, described how he and his friends had travelled to Grenoble for a motorcycle trial but ended up racing back through France for what was reported to be the last boat home.

Even as some Pomfretonians hurried home from Europe, many more were preparing to leave for France but a few still had thoughts about a more temporary departure. Mindful of the impact of the war on tourism, Blackpool Corporation placed adverts reminding holidaymakers that costs in the town were not rising and that 'Bread and provisions are as cheap as any town in England: Abundant Supply'. As the lucky few packed for the seaside, telegrams were arriving at the post office recalling Reservists to the army and navy and cyclist messengers were working full-time to ensure that men received their instructions for rejoining their regiments. It was a job made all the harder when seven of the sixteen postmen in the town were themselves recalled, one only a few days after his wedding. In the first week, around 130–150 local men were reported to have left to go back to the forces. At the Micklegate Ambulance Brigade Centre, twenty men responded to a call for volunteers for foreign service and an appeal was put out for anyone with first aid training to come forward to fill the gaps.

Since 1880, the barracks on the edge of town had housed the regimental depots of not one but two regiments. Now old soldiers of the King's Own Yorkshire Light Infantry (KOYLI) and the York and Lancaster Regiment began flooding into the town to report in, collect equipment and to be issued with travel warrants to enable them to reach their battalions.

> *It will readily be understood, therefore, that not only the railway station but also the town, and especially the barracks, were from Monday evening onwards scenes of interest, activity and in cases, of excitement.*

All large buildings in the area, including the Town Hall, the skating rink, the Territorial drill hall, and even local school classrooms, were taken over by the military to try to process men as quickly as possible. The plan was that men would be recalled to the colours and travel to Pontefract Barracks, where they would be held until a draft of around

Pontefract Barracks, built in 1880 as home to the King's Own Yorkshire Light Infantry and the York & Lancaster Regiments.

Pontefract barracks.

300 could be sent to reinforce the regiment's battalions. A measure of the practical problems this caused comes from the report that Mr C. Johnston, a baker in Tanshelf who held the contract to supply 1,000 loaves of bread per week to the barracks, was now being asked to provide 1,000 per day – not an easy task with flour prices increasing daily.

Hurriedly recalled from their summer camp at Whitby, the part-time soldiers of Castleford's Territorial Company of the 5th KOYLI reported to the drill hall for medical examinations. Three failed to meet the requirements for active service but the rest – 130 men – received orders to meet at 9.00am to march over to Pontefract and take the train to Doncaster, where the 1st West Riding (Territorial) Division was forming. 'It was generally thought that they would be leaving immediately,' the local paper reported, 'and a large crowd gathered to witness their departure, but they did not leave until three hours later and apart from making the necessary preparations they passed the time by singing ragtime songs and boxing and were generally "merry and bright".' It was not, the paper hastened to add, because they were not aware of their responsibilities, but that they were 'cheerfully ready and willing to do their duty to their country'. As the men, looking 'remarkably smart and fit', set out, crowds lined their route along Albion Street, Carlton Street and Pontefract Road on the first leg of a journey that would take them to France the following April.

Like most county regiments of the time, the full-time regular army battalions of the KOYLI were filled with men from all over the country and the 2nd Battalion (2 KOYLI) contained a sizeable contingent of men from as far afield as London, but most came from the industrial towns of the West Riding, especially from Sheffield and Leeds, with a few drawn from the area around the regiment's depot, and all had spent some time in Pontefract itself. Based in Dublin at the start of the war, the battalion was quickly sent out to join the British Expeditionary Force (BEF) in France, arriving at Le Havre on 16 August as part of 13th Brigade, 5th Division. They moved quickly into defensive positions along the Mons Canal where, on 21 August, Private John Parr of the Middlesex Regiment became the first British soldier to be killed in the war after his bicycle reconnaissance patrol clashed with a

Across the UK, crowds gathered to watch the local Territorials leave for war.

German unit near Obourg. By the next day, the BEF had 80,000 men in position awaiting the German attack that was expected at any time but it was, by European standards, a tiny force – a 'contemptible little army' as it was famously called. Nearly 60 per cent of its troops were men who had already served their time and left the forces only to be recalled at the outbreak of war after having settled into comfortable civilian jobs that meant they were by now out of shape and struggling to cope with a sudden return to active service. Most were out of practice in weapons drill and tactics. Their job now was to hold the canal line against a very large, very prepared, German army.

On the morning of 23 August, the main attack began. Massed formations of German troops advanced across open fields only to be met by withering rifle fire and were, according to one observer, 'mown down like grass'. Trained British soldiers could hit a man at a range of around 1,000 yards and fire fifteen aimed shots per minute, and even with so many men with rusty marksmanship skills, so deadly was the fire that Germans reported they were under attack from machine-guns. The first attack faltered and failed but the Germans came back again, more widely dispersed and in greater numbers. Slowly, the defenders were overwhelmed. By that afternoon, the British were ordered to fall back. The retreat from Mons had begun.

As the BEF retreated, units remained behind to hold off the Germans. On 26 August, it was the turn of 13th Brigade to make a stand at the village of Le Cateau. Like every battalion, 2 KOYLI kept an official War Diary:

> *Before 6.0. a.m. an order was received in the Brigadier-General's handwriting as follows:* "Orders have now been changed. There will be no retirement for the fighting troops. Fill up your trenches as far as possible with water, food and ammunition". *Later, Lieut-Colonel KINCAID-SMITH, of the II Army Corps Head-Quarters staff, rode up and repeated the order for* "no retirement". *This order was given to the signallers to be conveyed to all our Company Commanders, and Sergeant WILLINGTON, signalling sergeant, reported that this had been done.*

'No retirement for the fighting troops' meant only one thing. Lieutenant Butts, a young officer with the KOYLI, later recalled:

> *The* [Commanding Officers] *were summoned and the positions explained. The brigade was to be sacrificed to save the 5ᵗʰ Division. Our orders in the regiments were that we had to stay and fight it out to give the Division more time to get clear.*

By then, 2 KOYLI were on the right of a horseshoe-shaped defence line and it was not long before German cavalry appeared to scout out their position. Shortly afterwards, the enemy artillery opened a heavy bombardment and their infantry advanced. Fighting went on throughout the morning and into mid-afternoon with the British infantry driving off a series of determined attacks until, one by one, the battalions around the KOYLI were overrun by sheer weight of numbers. Despite the 'no retirement' order, by 1400hrs the situation was hopeless and the order for a fighting withdrawal was given. It is not clear whether Major Charles Allix Lavington 'Cal' Yate of 'B' Company ever received the order or if he decided to ignore it and fight on to give other troops the chance to withdraw. Whatever the truth, about two hours later the remnants of 'B' Company were surrounded on three sides and had all but run out of ammunition, with all the officers apart from Major Yate either dead or wounded. Refusing calls from the Germans to surrender, Major Yate rallied his nineteen remaining unwounded survivors (out of his original 220 men) and led a final, desperate bayonet charge against the massed German troops. It was a forlorn gesture but typical of the major's determination. He survived and was captured but died in captivity a few weeks later in circumstances that made it unclear whether he had been killed trying to escape or took his own life to avoid being recaptured during an escape attempt. In a letter written after the war the divisional commander, Sir Charles Fergusson, recalled 'it was mainly thanks to them (2 KOYLI) that the 2nd Corps was extricated that day and their stand is historic'. It came at a heavy cost. Eighteen of the battalion's twenty-six officers were killed, wounded or captured along with 582 of its 902 men. Pontefract Barracks became the scene of frantic activity as newly recalled reservists were rushed to France to replace 2 KOYLI's losses. Among them, 32-year-old Arthur Nettleship and John Parkin of Whitwood, both former KOYLI men who had thought their soldiering days were behind them. Nettleship had only recently left the army after service in Hong Kong, but like thousands of others was now hastily collecting equipment and awaiting transport to France.

These men would join a unit still heavily engaged in holding back the German advance toward Paris. Some sense of the fighting comes from the battalion War Diary of 26 October:

Very heavy shell firing on our trenches today from early morning. D [Company's] *trench was badly broken up for 40 yards. Men were buried alive. Capt R W S STANTON was wounded in the thigh by a piece of shell. The shelling consisted chiefly of so-called "Jack Johnsons"* [a German shell that exploded in a cloud of black smoke and named after an African-American boxing champion of the time] ... *17 men were killed and about 40 wounded.*

That night, 149 men and three officers of a new draft arrived and were rushed straight into the trenches. Of the officers leading the draft,

Second Lieutenant Carswell of the Reserve Battalion at Pontefract would be killed and his colleague, Second Lieutenant Shannon, would be 'sent home sick' within twenty-four hours of arriving at the front. As the diary explains, events of 28–29 October were no improvement:

> *Still in trenches. Heavy shell firing and heavy casualties. Capt RICHMOND killed. "A" [Company's] trenches got worst of shelling – though other Companies had their share. Capt CARTER's trench lost 9 killed and about 12 wounded, French Artillery firing short amounted for a great many of these – the same trench resisted a frontal attack at 12:00 noon and enemy returned to trenches at 7:00pm 500 yards away.*

Edwin Davis, a new arrival from South Milford, was among those killed. Charles Parkinson from Pontefract died on 31 October, and Arthur Nettleship on 1 November. It would not be until December that George English's family in Temple Street, Castleford, would hear of his fate, when a postcard arrived from a German hospital. George and his officer had been blasted off their feet by a shell around 31 October while trying to deliver a message. Both wounded, they had been blown into an abandoned section of trench where they lay for two days without food or water until found by German stretcher-bearers. George was well, he told them, but very lonely as he was the only British soldier in a ward full of wounded Germans, although he said he was being treated well.

Meanwhile, Pontefract-born Michael Hector McGuirk, a colour sergeant originally from 2 KOYLI, was involved in a very different war. Under the command of Major General C.M. Dobell, he was part of a force landed at Douala and Victoria on the coast of Cameroon in West Africa on 27 September to try to clear the German-led troops occupying the area. The Germans pulled back to the town of Jabassi, and it was decided to use the Wuri river to launch an attack by boat. Six companies of the West African Rifles and two from the Nigerian Regiment, along with another from the Gold Coast Regiment and about 100 Royal Navy sailors and marines were assigned the task. Seconded to the West African Rifles, Hector McGuirk sailed with them on a barge up the Wuri river and landed about 5 kilometres from Jabassi. They marched through thick jungle that broke the units into small groups so that, when the attack started, German defenders were able to force them to retreat back into the bush. When a second attack also failed, the troops were ordered back to Douala, but it was too late for Hector McGuirk. He was killed on 8 October leading his men, one of twenty-six Europeans to die in a battle almost unnoticed at the time and which a century later remains almost completely forgotten.

Britain ruled over a vast empire and these small campaigns were a reminder of just how much manpower would be needed to cope with the demands of fighting a major war in Europe while protecting its widespread interests abroad. As 1 KOYLI left Singapore, for example, the Ottoman Empire declared Jihad against the British, leading to a short but brutal mutiny against British rule by Muslim troops of the Indian Army brought in to replace them. Forces were also needed to maintain order in India itself, where nationalists were agitating against British rule. British naval supply bases were threatened by German troops active in West Africa and thousands of Allied soldiers would become embroiled in a guerrilla war against a German force in East Africa. British troops would be called upon to join an Anglo-Japanese attack on the German defenders of the port of Tsingtao in China in November 1914. Realising that this would not be a short war and that Britain's tiny professional army could never hope to last long against the huge numbers of troops Germany could call upon in France, let alone manage its other commitments around the globe, the newly appointed Secretary of State for War, Lord Kitchener, set out to create a New Army, appealing first for 100,000 volunteers to come forward. Brought up to believe in the importance of Britain's empire, young men keen for adventure flocked to the colours. By 21 August, Pontefract reported recruiting around 100 men per day and a cheering crowd gathered for a charity football match at Lock Lane heard that Castleford had produced a larger percentage of recruits than any other town in the country.

Fifteen years earlier, the British Army had struggled to produce enough manpower to contain the Boers in South Africa, even though thousands of volunteers had come forward to enlist. The authorities were shocked by the numbers of potential recruits failing the army's most basic fitness requirements, leading to claims that the British race was becoming too unfit to manage an overseas empire. In response, the government agreed the establishment of a committee on physical deterioration in 1903 to examine the problem. The findings were deeply worrying. The Acland Report of 1906 heard of childminders who routinely dosed children in their care with opium and of children fainting from hunger at school. Bradford had become the first education authority to address the issue by providing school meals, initially funded personally by staff but later (and technically illegally) by school funds. Liberal reforms aimed at improving the welfare of the nation were brought in and very quickly, studies showed an improvement in health and achievement at school but it was not enough. In 1913, the medical officer for Batley reported that on average, children of 13 had the physique he would expect of an 11-year-old. Physical defects linked to poor nutrition were the norm. Dental problems were so common as to not be worth recording except in cases where children had reasonably healthy teeth and infestations of head and body lice in some schools ran at 100 per cent. For generations of pit workers, deprived of vitamins by a poor diet and of sunlight and fresh air by the effects of local industries, the problems were even worse.

In the rush to volunteer in 1914, many found themselves rejected for what seemed trivial reasons: bad teeth would affect their ability to chew the notoriously solid army rations and meant they were deemed unfit for service but some got around this by having all their teeth removed. It may not have helped with chewing but it got them around the reason for rejection. Others might be rejected because a speech impediment was thought to affect their ability to pass messages. Some of the newly forming battalions were intended to ensure that the 'right sort' were allowed to join and volunteers might be admitted based on their father's occupation rather than their own physical condition. In fact, so many came forward that the army could afford to be very selective, to the point of raising its minimum height requirement to 5 feet 6 inches in order to limit the numbers applying. Many hundreds of men tried repeatedly to volunteer, only to face continual rejection.

Unfortunately for them, the patriotic fervour that had gripped the

Recruits swear the oath of allegiance. Next step was to accept 'the King's shilling' as their first day's pay.

A new batch of volunteers for the New Army being inspected before setting out to join their new regiment.

nation paid little heed to why a man wasn't in uniform, only the fact that he wasn't. Any man of military age seen in civilian clothes could draw the attention of recruiting sergeants or bands of young women who had taken to presenting white feathers as a symbol of cowardice to anyone they suspected of being 'a shirker'. With enthusiasm taking priority over evidence, men in essential occupations, others who had been rejected by the army, and even wounded soldiers home on convalescent leave, found themselves branded cowards and accused of failing their duty to the country. In response, the government began issuing special lapel badges for those whose work at home was more valuable than service overseas. So many specialist workers had enlisted that war production was affected and the government began retrieving men with essential skills from the forces to return to their civilian jobs wearing military uniform.

Across the country, those men who were unable to enlist because of their responsibilities at home or who had been turned away from army medicals were nevertheless keen to serve in some way. In the years leading up to war, newspapers had been filled with stories of German agents and of the ability of the German military to transport men by Zeppelin to attack anywhere in the country. With the British Army overstretched by the fighting in France and Belgium, fears began to grow around how men could protect their own homes in case of an enemy invasion, a fear stoked by William Le Queux's bestselling *The Invasion of 1910*. Written in 1906, the book was a phenomenal success and translated into almost thirty languages worldwide. Written as a military history, it told the story of a German invasion of England and began with a landing at Goole. Troops from Pontefract were the first sent to counter the attack and the story describes the advance south towards Doncaster and the eventual takeover of the West Riding. Just one of around 200 novels and short stories, the British people had been conditioned to believe an invasion was not only possible but likely – a fear that would still hold strong as late as 1918.

The answer to the threat came from Ireland where, with the issue of home rule threatening to spark a civil war, Irishmen had banded together into armed civilian groups like the Ulster Volunteer Force. Using their example, and despite the fact that they were technically illegal, groups like Castleford's Civilian Training Corps sprang up. In their own time and at their own expense, volunteers came forward to provide a home defence force that would become the model for the Second World War's Home Guard. Unable to stop their enthusiastic efforts, the War Office finally gave in and allowed the Volunteer Training Corps to be organised by a central committee. At first only allowed to wear a red armband emblazoned with the letters GR (standing for Georgius Rex and showing they were on official war service), the new part-time soldiers did what they could. Some boasted a great deal of experience – one recruit was 80 and had attended fifty-two summer camps with the old Militia – others brought optimistic enthusiasm rather than military ability. Many invested 10 shillings in a dummy rifle to stand guard over railways and other important targets

Those rejected for military service due to age, infirmity or personal circumstances enlisted into the Volunteer Training Corps – the forerunner to WW2's 'Dad's Army' of the Home Guard.

for any lurking spies, because the 12,000 volunteers across the West Riding could manage just 750 working rifles between them. When the Castleford Corps was disbanded, it had just one to be shared by the whole company. Little wonder that many joked that the armband stood for Gorgeous Wrecks.

Everyone, it seemed, wanted to do their bit to protect their homes. Among the first to be mobilised were the local boy scouts with an advert appearing in the local paper announcing that the eighteen troops in the Pontefract and Castleford area were available to help in a variety of roles, from labouring to bring in the harvest to providing clerks and messengers to the military and local authorities. Shortly afterwards, Miss Margaret Andrews of Ackworth informed the local paper that as honorary secretary of the National Union of Women's Suffrage Societies, she could assure the government that suffragists had 'not only suspended their ordinary political work but are preparing to use the entire organisation for the help of those who will be sufferers from the economic and industrial dislocation caused by the war'.

With two regiments sharing the barracks on the edge of town, soon Pontefract was swamped as recruits flooded in for the New Army forming in response to Lord Kitchener's appeal for volunteers. Prepared and equipped to manage up to 30,000 recruits in a year, the British Army found itself with almost a million by Christmas 1914, creating chaos at all regimental depots but particularly at Pontefract where the rapidly expanding KOYLI and York and Lancaster regiments shared the limited space available. Not surprisingly, supplies of beds, uniforms, equipment and even food soon began to run out. Some men were billeted with local families, others in any available buildings, while more slept in tents pitched around the barracks as the harassed depot staff struggled to maintain any sort of order. Many men simply walked away and went home for their meals or to visit families for the weekend, often without their absence being noticed. Those who lived too far away stayed put and complaints began to appear in local papers about conditions at the depot. On 26 September, under the heading 'Life at Pontefract Camp – Silly Rumours Contradicted', the *Dewsbury Reporter* received a letter from a group of local men:

Fear of attacks by German agents on 'vulnerable points' meant that boy scouts were widely deployed as guards.

ITALIAN WOMEN ARE
SERVING THEIR COUNTRY
WHY CAN'T WE

Suffragists and suffragettes saw the war as a chance to show that they could contribute more than knitting and nursing.

Many rumours have been circulated in the district regarding the conditions under which our local soldiers are housed at Pontefract and the treatment they have received with regard to food etc. The following letter has come to hand this week, and we trust that it will put an end to the ridiculous tales: "To the Editor of the Reporter, Sir, – Having heard that there have been many rumours about that the Pontefract camp is in a filthy condition and that there is not enough to eat for the soldiers, we, the undersigned, wish to contradict these rumours. We are all Batley chaps who have been at Pontefract for three weeks, and we are all in the pink of condition and ready for anything. The camp is cleared up and disinfected every day, and as for eating, we have enough and to spare. For breakfast we have bread and butter – not margarine – and jam and cheese; for dinner we have boiled beef, fresh every day, along with cabbage and carrots; and for tea we get bread and butter, tinned salmon and tinned herrings or potted beef: so you will see whether we are pined or not".

Local trader George Hemmant was again in the paper for his efforts to help, setting up breakfasts at the Butter Cross every morning between 5.30am and 7.30am for recruits billeted in town. Aided by two scouts who reported at 5am every morning, meals were provided at cost price and up to 250 men per day made their way there. Despite the inevitable complaints from a minority, for many young men from poorer backgrounds the army diet – with meat every day – was the best food they had ever had. Studies found recruits growing an average of an extra two inches in height and gaining up to a stone in weight during their basic training thanks to a healthy diet and exercise. For enthusiastic young volunteers from the professional classes, the

At the overcrowded camps, new recruits for the army found themselves living out in the open. Their first military task was often to build a camp to house themselves.

Early recruits to Kitchener's New Army often served their first few weeks wearing the clothes they had enlisted in.

introduction to army life was a hard one and grumbles about conditions continued, although their new comrades from the working classes regarded it as something of a holiday.

Slowly, Kitchener's New Army began to take shape but after the initial rush, and perhaps because of rumours about camp life, recruiting began to fall off. It was then that a suggestion was put forward that men might like to serve alongside 'the right sort of comrade', and recruiting began for what would become known as 'Pals' battalions. Men from particular areas or trades could enlist to serve together and not to have to mix with ordinary soldiers in what one observer said should be seen 'as much as a social club as a military unit'. With facilities available in the UK for up to 175,000 men of the regular army in July 1914, finding room for almost a million six months later was a major problem, but still more would be needed. Yet although thousands volunteered, they represented only a small proportion of the men available. Many were held back by practical issues around providing for their families, but others were simply reluctant to join an army still widely regarded as being a refuge for the desperate, inhabited by men Wellington had called the 'scum of the earth'.

As one letter to the *Hull Daily Mail* explained:

> *Are we not patriotic in Hull? Whether we are or not, the fact remains that recruiting for the army, so far as Hull is concerned, is very poor. I cannot think that the shocking response to Lord Kitchener's appeal is due to either indifference or to cowardice. There must be a reason why young men are holding back. A friend of mine, a few days ago, expressed his intention of enlisting, he now states he will not do so unless more of his own class volunteer. What my friend is suggesting is this: that instead of some of the larger employers of labour in Hull giving big donations of money they should use their influence to organize Corps of the middle class young men – clerks, tailors, drapers' assistants, grocers, assistants, warehousemen and artisans. Then we should see men living, sleeping and training in company of others of their own class. It is the idea of having to herd with all types of men now being enlisted that keeps our young athletes and men of good birth and training from joining the colours. At least that is the opinion I have gathered from conversation with likely candidates.*

Such sentiments were being expressed across the country and General Sir Henry Rawlinson, thinking along similar lines, suggested they might be more inclined to enlist if they knew they were going to serve alongside their friends and work colleagues. He experimented with an appeal to raise a battalion of men from workers in the City of London to set an example and, within a week, 1,600 men enlisted in the 10th (Service) Battalion, Royal Fusiliers – the so-called Stockbrokers' Battalion. A few days later, the Earl of Derby set out to raise a battalion of men from Liverpool and, within two days, 1,500 Liverpudlians had joined what Lord Derby told them 'should be a battalion of pals, a battalion in which friends from the same office will fight shoulder to shoulder for the honour of Britain and the credit of Liverpool'. Over the next few days, still more came forward, enough for three more battalions. Encouraged by this spectacular success, Kitchener encouraged similar recruitment campaigns and soon towns and cities were vying to outdo each other in forming their own local battalions. The idea was that wealthy individuals, local authorities or committees would raise their own battalions then feed, house and train them until they could be handed over to the War Office as a formed unit.

Among the groups attempting to raise their own battalion was the West Yorkshire Coal Owners Association, who put aside £22,000 for the purpose and began recruiting at pits across Yorkshire, but struggled to find enough men willing to join what was already being referred to as the Pontefract Battalion. Many miners had already enlisted but many more fell foul of the new regulations raising the minimum height requirement from 5 feet 2 inches to 5 feet 6 inches. Given the difficulties, the WYCOA considered simply donating £10,000 to the War Office instead, but when they approached them the War Office agreed to waive the rules and to draft in extra numbers from among the other KOYLI volunteers provided they would be treated the same as their former miner comrades. It also offered to provide £7 5s per man for equipment and 2 shillings a day for food. Thus encouraged, the WYCOA went back to recruiting what was now being referred to as the 12th (Service) Battalion (Yorkshire Miner's) of the King's Own Yorkshire Light Infantry or, more simply, 12th KOYLI. By the end of the year, a full battalion was in training at Farnley Park near Leeds.

Some pals battalions drew from a broad cross-section of their communities but many others restricted admittance, as E. Robinson found when he attempted to join the Leeds Pals:

On September 3 I went down to Leeds Town Hall to join the local branch – i.e. Leeds Pals – of the West Yorks Regiment ... The main hall of the Town Hall had about sixty young fellows arguing rather excitedly, but I and a fellow whom I had told my intention to and was joining me, went up to a table at the top of the room where two or three well dressed, prosperous looking gents were seated. I was asked what my father did for a living, much to my surprise, and I suggested I wanted to join and not my father. I said I was a clerk, but they insisted I should say what my father did. It was curiouser and curiouser, but eventually I said he was a farm worker. Very politely, very firmly, it was told to me that only professional men's sons, or whose fathers had businesses, could join for a day or two – it was exclusive. My friend promptly nudged me and said he was going about his job, he never did join up ... well my patriotism wasn't very deep, and Belgian atrocities didn't cut much ice, but I was fearfully sick of a humdrum life that led nowhere and promised nothing, so I went to another recruiting depot and was enlisted as a gunner in the [Royal Artillery].

In Hull, men from the commercial sector formed a battalion for themselves, tradesmen another, sportsmen a third, and anyone not eligible for those options could try for the fourth battalion, known simply as 't'Others'. Raised not by the War Office but by local committees, pals recruits had a slightly easier time of their first few weeks in the military, often living at home and training by day in local parks or drill halls. But whatever type of unit they joined, young men had rushed to enlist expecting to be processed through training and off to France very quickly. It didn't happen. As the system broke down under the enormous pressure, men got bored and sought out whatever entertainment could be found, leading to one local citizen to complain that the young men hanging around Pontefract were 'a rowdy lot' compared to the Germans he had seen in Brussels as he made his way home at the start of the war. The comments prompted an angry response from another reader who pointed out that 'it is not easy for thousands of young men to remain sedate in a town which has over twenty licenced premises within 200 yards of the Parish Church', and that they were, on the whole, well-behaved. It helped, of course, that the government had passed the draconian Defence of the Realm Act. A short piece of legislation rushed through immediately war broke out, DORA, as it became known, allowed the government to impose any restrictions it saw fit and would come to affect the lives of every single person in the country. Among DORA's powers was the right to restrict the sale of alcohol and pubs deemed to be in military areas around barracks, dockyards and munitions plants fell under its control. Opening times were cut from the pre-war 5.30am opening and selling until around midnight to a ruling they could only serve soldiers between noon and 1.00pm and from 6.00 to 9.00pm. The rules, though, did not apply to clubs, leading to bitter arguments between pub landlords and club stewards about how the rules should be applied.

With nothing much to do and nowhere to entertain themselves when off-duty, bored soldiers began to desert in order to enlist in other regiments where the prospects seemed better. Others simply tagged on to drafts of men being sent off to training camps around the country and hoped no one would notice the extra bodies. Posted from Tralee in Ireland to Pontefract Barracks, Captain Godfrey Drage of the Royal Munster Fusiliers decided to use the chaos there to his own regiment's advantage:

> *I realised that I had very little idea how many men the Munsters could possibly absorb. However a thousand seemed a good round number and so I announced, "I'm only authorised to take a thousand of you". Then I made them strip to the waist and walked down the ranks feeling each man's biceps and asking what he was in civil life. If he said "I'm a miner" I took him without more ado. So far I'd got away with everything but, by the time I'd got five hundred lined up the Adjutant of the depot heard about my goings on and came running up – "Here I say Captain Drage, you can't do that! You're taking all my best men". I thought I'd better not ride my luck too far and so I saluted very subserviently and replied, "Yes sir, certainly sir, would you like to choose the rest yourself sir?" He did so and you can imagine what the next five hundred were like. Anyway, I'd got my draft and thought I'd better be off while the going was good.*

More were poached for the Connaught Rangers, while 500 more who had signed up for the KOYLI or the York and Lancasters had served only a week before they allowed themselves to be talked out of the army altogether and poached to serve as infantry in the newly formed Royal Naval Division, marching proudly out of Pontefract led by the church boys' brigade band. Gradually, though, the system began to work itself out. As more and more battalions of the KOYLI and York and Lancasters were formed, drafts of around 300 men each were put together and sent on their way to camps scattered around the country.

By the end of August, the BEF, made up in large part of the reservists hastily recalled at the outbreak of war, was in full retreat. It had been pushed back from Mons and had headed south, reaching the lines of the Aisne and Marne valleys north of Paris itself. At the end of September, news arrived of the area's first casualties. On 22 September, Private 7899 Ernest Hinchliffe from Castleford was killed in fighting on the River Aisne when the 1st Battalion of the West Yorkshire Regiment were overrun by the German attack. Two days later, Private 7776 Joseph Morran of Lingard Yard in Ferrybridge died of wounds sustained when the Coldstream Guards held another sector of the Aisne Front. In the chaos of the retreat, hundreds of men were listed as missing and, from time to time, postcards arrived to let families know that a man had been wounded or captured and was alive. Week after week families waited anxiously for news.

Somehow, the battered British and French forces held on and prevented the Germans reaching Paris. Both sides dug trenches to hold their positions. Realising that each needed to outflank the other, now began what historians refer to as 'the race to the sea', as each side threw forces into the front line to extend the trench lines as far as possible in order to prevent the other being able to slip around the side of their flanks. By the end of the year, trenches ran from the Belgian coast to the Swiss border and neither side had gained an advantage. The trench stalemate had begun.

November brought news of the death of another Castleford man, 36-year-old former labourer John Smith, who had been serving on coastal defence duties in Sunderland. Smith had joined the York and Lancaster Regiment at Pontefract on 10 August and had been sent to form part of the Tyneside garrison. On 11 November, the battalion commander had issued orders confining the men to the Coastguard Drill Hall on Featherstone Street and armed guards were on patrol outside. At about 1pm, Private Flynn handed his loaded weapon to his relief, Private Haines. What happened next was never fully explained but at about 2.45pm Smith decided to sneak out for some reason. Guard commander Lance-Corporal Porter heard the sound of a rifle shot and ran out onto the street where he found Smith lying on the footpath, bleeding from a wound in his neck. An inquest was held the next day before Coroner J.F. Burnicle, when it was revealed Smith had been shot while trying to leave the hall without permission. Witness Edith Coulson told him: 'I was in the street when the shot was fired. I saw a soldier fall to the ground. The sentry said he hadn't known the rifle was loaded.' Summing up the case, the coroner remarked that there was no evidence of any grudge between Haines and Smith and that the sentry had simply been doing his duty. A verdict of death by misadventure was returned and all military records pertaining to John Smith's death were later marked as 'accidental'.

In early December, some of the men who had gone straight to war in August came home on leave, bringing with them the first indications of what was happening in France. Sergeant Major John Moore had been with 2nd KOYLI during the retreat and came home to Pontefract, where he described what he had seen to the *Yorkshire Post*:

> *For six days, from October 23, they were in the trenches under terrible conditions, and in this time the "D" Company alone had 25 killed, 40 wounded and one missing, and three poor fellows went mad ...* [When relieved by Gurkhas] *they reached their "resting place" [where] there was an urgent message for help from General E. H. Allenby, who was in charge of a cavalry corps near Messines. Motors were waiting, and the "Koylis", the King's Own Scottish Borderers, the Northumberland Fusiliers and the Lincolns – four battalions in all – were sent to the cavalry's aid. A few minutes after their arrival at Neuve Eglise they were once more engaged with the enemy at close quarters, and with fixed bayonets. Here the "Koylis" suffered over 300 casualties and nearly every officer fell.*

Despite such news, by the end of the year the initial shock of war had passed and life was returning to some sort of normality. The fear of imminent invasion had waned and once again the people of Britain began to feel safe behind the English Channel, knowing that the Royal Navy was the strongest in the world and could protect them from any attack by sea. By late 1914, though, the Royal Navy was thinly stretched. A major sea battle off the Falkland Islands in early December and the need to patrol the North Atlantic had depleted the Grand Fleet and the Germans knew it. Although a seaborne invasion was out of the question, raiding operations were planned to draw out and trap ships of the Royal Navy either alone or, ideally, to have a small force of ships give chase so that they could be lured out to seas where the German High Fleet would be waiting. Raids along the British coast might also have the effect of making the British split the powerful Grand Fleet so it could guard ports along the whole of the East Coast, making it easier to attack.

Trenches dug on the Yorkshire coast as a defence against the expected German invasion.

A small raid off Great Yarmouth in November led to the sinking of a British submarine, but by December the Germans were ready for something bigger. Early on the morning of the 16th, German ships began shelling the east coast, hitting Hartlepool, Scarborough and Whitby with over a thousand shells and killing or wounding around 600 people. Sydney Smith recalled what happened:

I was seven years and five days old. It was a misty morning. We were up early before school. And my mother was in the act of putting the porridge out for us onto the plates when the first shell cracked. My mother said, "Oh, what's that noise?" My father said, "It's gunfire, it'll be alright it'll be some of our ships practising." Never dreamt it would be Germans. As soon as it was over I went out and went round the corner to see if school was still there – unfortunately it was!

Thomas Darbyshire, a Territorial Force soldier in hospital at Scarborough, recalled how people began crying, '"The Germans are landing! The Germans are landing!" I did not feel apprehensive or excited. I just felt that the time I'd trained for had come and I was quite calm and quite prepared for anything that might have been going to happen.' Meanwhile, Colina Campbell, a 23-year old Voluntary Aid Detachment worker, also heard the gunfire. As she wrote later:

Suddenly at 9.10am we heard what the children thought was blasting, only very near, the windows rattled and the house shook again and again. I said "I am sure it's firing off the coast" ... I can tell you the sound was pretty terrifying but it only lasted ten minutes, the car was ordered and away we flew to Whitby. We were there about three-quarters of an hour after the two German cruisers had gone but the houses they had wrecked were awful. When we got near Whitby we saw streams of people with panic stricken faces trying to get away. I never want to see such a thing again ... Telegraph wires hanging like threads all snapped, huge gaping holes in the side of houses, roofs off, glass smashed everywhere and old women shaking with fright and sobbing. We picked up lots of bits of shell. I have one in my pocket as I write.

The two German cruisers fired at the coastguard station, shot that to bits and killed one coastguard; we saw the stretcher being carried. Some of the coastguards said the cruisers came in so close they could see the men working on their decks. We hear that these cruisers have visited Scarborough and other places and damaged them, but as all wires are out of order it is difficult to get news. In one street the venetian blinds had been blown right across the street, lamp post upturned and I saw a pool of blood in front of a house so went in to see if anyone was hurt. We found that an old woman had been hit by a shell and was bleeding badly and was removed to the hospital. The extraordinary thing was so few were killed or even badly hurt. Portions of furniture, doors and windows were lying about the streets, and in the fields just outside the town are large holes about five or six feet square. If the shells had been fired earlier when people were in bed I should think hundreds would have been killed as so many of the bedrooms were struck.

An artist's impression of the shelling of Scarborough, December 1914.

Shelling damage, Scarborough. The attack on a resort so many knew from childhood convinced many that Germany intended to destroy the British way of life.

The next day's *Yorkshire Post* reported that the shelling had been heard as far away as Tadcaster but that 'there was nothing that could be described as panic' among the civilian population of Scarborough, although 'the railway station was besieged' by people fleeing the town. Soon, York and Leeds were filled with refugees, some 'half clothed' with only what they had been wearing at the time the bombardment started, others carrying large bundles of luggage. Meanwhile, as some fled, others boarded excursion trains, 'evidently considering a display of shell fire an added attraction', and went to view the damage. The attack on Hartlepool had been the most costly in terms of lives and damage but it was the shelling of a seaside resort so well-known to thousands that caused the real outrage and soon 'Remember Scarborough!' became a recruiting slogan across the country.

It was a potent reminder that with ships and Zeppelins capable of reaching Britain, the country was no longer safe from the effects of war in Europe. This was only a raid but invasion remained a real risk. Recruiting for the army increased but so too did recruiting for the local

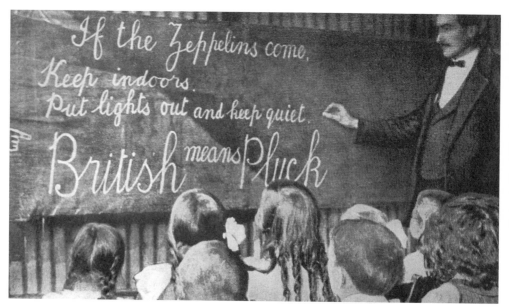

Schoolchildren being taught emergency drills in case of air-raid.

volunteers. On the day after the raid, Major Ellis of the York and Lancaster Regiment was invited to inspect the Pontefract Athlete's Volunteer Training Force and found an average of seventy men attending nightly drill sessions under the leadership of local solicitor Commandant Claude Guy Leatham and Instructor Sergeant Thomas. 'There was no doubt,' Ellis told them, 'that large bodies of men over military age would be mobilised for home defence, or as Special Constables,' and that their training made them extremely valuable to their country.

Shortly before Christmas, the Pontefract Workhouse received news that the Local Government Board had agreed to pay £13 5s as half the costs of maintaining the wives and families of German miners working in Featherstone at the start of the war and now interned in prison camps. The clerk for Pontefract's board of guardians reported that he had 'gone through all the formalities to secure their return to Germany', and appeared miffed that the women had refused to go, preferring to stay with friends in Featherstone rather than leave their husbands and homes. Unfortunately, there had been complaints about 'hunwives' and efforts were continuing to 'compel them to return to Germany'.

If Christmas spirit towards the wives and children of former workmates was lacking, shopkeepers reported that, despite shortages, sales were healthy as households stocked up with whatever was available. As they had since October, the patrons of Castleford's Smawthorne Hotel continued to raise £1 a week to send tobacco and other gifts out to local men in France. Meanwhile, Katherine Shaw, Mayoress of Pontefract, appealed to the Christmas spirit by asking for coats and boots for the Reserve Battalion of the 5th KOYLI to help out until winter clothing could be issued. The Yorkshire Miners Association reported that it had already dealt with thirty-seven death claims paid for men who had been killed on active service and announced it would no longer require members who were serving in the forces to pay contributions.

Bad news, though, came just at Christmas itself when Colonel Howe, as commandant of the Pontefract Depot, used his power under the Defence of the Realm Act to order all pubs and clubs in Pontefract and the surrounding areas to close at 9pm every evening starting on Christmas Eve, and to be closed to men in uniform except between noon and 1pm and 6pm to 9pm. The order was not well-received, especially since, according to local reports, 'during the Christmas season there were not more than fifty or so soldiers quartered in the town'.

CHAPTER 2

Hunwives and Belgian Atrocities

After the initial chaos of the war's outbreak, by the beginning of 1915 things were becoming more settled. Armed police still guarded certain places considered to be targets for 'organised gangs of enemy aliens', but although the expected uprising of Eastern European immigrants had failed to materialise it was still a difficult time to be a foreigner in Britain. Many immigrants were Jews forced out of their homes by the political situation in their homelands who had arrived in Britain throughout the previous century. Thousands had become naturalised British citizens and some had even served in the British Army. Hundreds had married British women and considered themselves to be at home. The outbreak of war, though, made them all potential enemies in the eyes of local communities.

In the first few days of war, the British Government allowed free passage to any immigrants of military age recalled to their old regiments, allowing hundreds of German and Austrian reservists to leave the country, almost certainly to fight against Britain. Attention then turned to those who stayed and, late in 1914, police and soldiers began rounding up men of military age whose families came from Germany, Austria or Hungary, or who were unable to produce evidence of their nationality – including at least one stray Australian who found himself the sole English speaker in a prison full of German ex-pats.

Germans living in Britain, including local miners, were rounded up and sent to internment camps like that at Lofthouse near Wakefield.

Around the country special camps were set-up in whatever accommodation could be found to house those deemed a potential risk. Alexandra Palace in North London was taken over as a temporary prison, while others found themselves living in stables at Newbury racecourse. Those interned from the Yorkshire area might, if they were lucky, find themselves at Lofthouse Park near Wakefield, where a prison camp had been created by erecting an electric fence around the entertainment complex that had been built there a few years earlier. Soon, crowds gathered to watch trainloads of 'enemy aliens' arrive at Wakefield stations and be packed onto trams for the journey to the camp. Across the North Sea, similar scenes were played out in Germany where British sailors, businessmen, students and others unable to leave the country in time were imprisoned in camps there.

Although the camp at Lofthouse was considered to be comfortable (prisoners had to agree to pay rent to be assigned there), it was still imprisonment and no one could predict how long it would be for.

Conditions at Lofthouse internment camp were considered so good that prisoners paid rent to be assigned there.

Interned German civilians at Alexandra Palace, London.

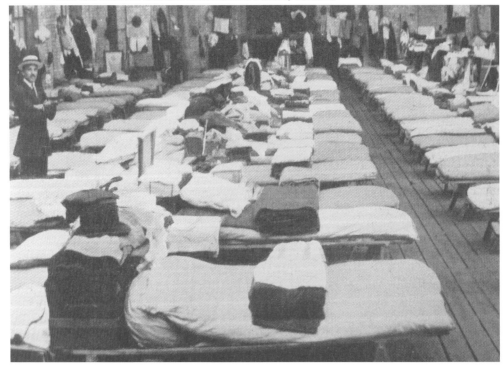

Behind them, the prisoners left their homes and their businesses, but most of all their English-born wives and children. Under the terms of the 1870 Naturalization Act, any woman marrying a foreign man automatically lost her British citizenship and took her husband's nationality. Now, women and children who had never set foot outside their own country found themselves listed as 'enemy aliens' or 'hunwives'. With their husbands gone, they struggled to support their families and risked separation in the workhouse if they failed. For one group of wives of German-born miners arrested at Featherstone, this would become a long-running battle.

Even as some foreigners were sent to what were referred to what was, at the time, the harmless term 'concentration camps', others were welcomed into the country with open arms. The papers had been full of horror stories of atrocities committed during the German advance into Belgium and packed with lurid accounts of rape and pillage. Certainly there had been incidents of mass murder, and the destruction of the town of Louvain had been deliberate and criminal, but the press – unable to fill their pages with real war news because of press censorship – were more than willing to print any story without question or evidence. A Scottish nurse from Dumfries, 23-year-old Grace Hume,

German civilians being marched into captivity. Despite the smiles, their families faced the workhouse and, in some cases, it would be years before they would see each other again.

became a national heroine after she had tried to defend her patients from German troops. After her capture, her right breast was cut off and she was left to die. Later, a nurse named Millard described how Grace shot one of her attackers before being taken. The story ran for almost two weeks before a somewhat confused Grace Hume pointed out that reports of her torture and death were slightly exaggerated given that she had never been to Belgium and was, in fact, working at a hospital in Huddersfield at the time of the alleged atrocity. No witness named Millard was ever found and the story was eventually traced back to the overactive imagination of Grace's 17-year-old sister.

Despite this, people were only too willing to believe any rumour, especially about the behaviour of the Germans in 'plucky little Belgium'. Forced out of their homes, thousands of refugees flooded westward and, by the end of 1914, an estimated 250,000 had arrived at the port of Folkestone with around 16,000 arriving on 14 October 1914 alone. Soon, housing Belgian refugees became not just a valuable service, but a competitive sport. Collections began around Castleford and Pontefract to raise money to help and smokers were encouraged to save the lead wrappers of their cigarettes, which could then be collected and sold, allowing people to 'enjoy your smoke … and do something for the brave Belgian people'. In October, the Castleford Catholic Women's League were busy preparing a house at 26 Ferrybridge Road, donated by local man John Austin, for the arrival of two families of Belgian refugees and they expected a total of twelve people. Not to be outdone, the Congregationalists obtained 'one of the Corporation's working class dwellings' and hoped to be able to pay the rent and provide 25 shillings a week to the 'guests'. As soon as the property was ready, they confidently reported, 'a party of refugees will be sent from Leeds'. In December, a committee formed in Pontefract was a little disappointed not to have got any yet but had not only prepared two houses already, but had a third on standby and a clothing and food depot established in Ropergate. Finally, eighteen refugees were delivered to Tanshelf Station:

In one house are a family from Eernighen, five in number, the head of whom was a director of a brewery. In the same house

26 Ferrybridge Road, Castleford. Home to some of the area's Belgian refugees.

*are also a mother (a dressmaker) and daughter from Ostend. In
a second house are lodged a wood carver and his wife and son
from Malines, a mother and daughter from the same town and
an electrician from Aerschott. In the third house are a waiter
and his wife from Andremont, a labourer and his wife from La
Reid and a man who is alone who was a spinner when in
Belgium.*

Shortly behind Pontefract's new arrivals came a report that between
thirty-five and forty refugees would be accommodated at Red Hill
House in Castleford by the Local Distress Committee, but by early
1915 the flood had reduced to a trickle. For a time, housing a refugee
was fashionable and some were treated almost as pets. Local people

were urged not to buy drinks for them because Belgians were thought to be unable to cope with the strength of British beer – although the makers of Stella Artois seem to have got their revenge in the long run. After a time, the standard joke between those who had housed their charges was to ask, 'and how are your Belgian atrocities?'

The refugees had sometimes been carefully picked. Belgium's mining communities were badly affected and many pit workers found themselves forced out of their homes by the fighting around the main coalfield areas, but unions in Britain had made it clear they would not be welcome if they tried to find work that could be done by a British miner. It was a tricky situation for the refugees to be in. On the one hand, their hosts soon became less enthusiastic about supporting the fit and healthy refugees financially when they were capable of working to support themselves, but at the same time they were warned against taking jobs away from local people. Only after a great deal of debate was it agreed in December 1915 that 'no further objection is to be raised by the Miners' Federation of Great Britain to the employment of Belgians underground provided that they are practical miners, understand English and receive trade union rates of wages'. As more and more men went into the army, the manpower shortage became so acute that Belgians began to find work opportunities opening up for them and over 6,000 were employed in a single shell factory near Twickenham. Employment, though, was not the only problem issue. It was known that Belgians ate horse meat. Local committees met to consider allowing certain butchers to be licenced to sell it and, later in the war when food supplies were running low, even to extend these licences to all butchers but, hard though it is to imagine happening today, there were fears that unscrupulous butchers might try to pass it off as beef.

The fact that enemy aliens were white and often spoke with local accents while 'plucky Belgians' were white and had foreign accents, made life for the narrow-minded more complicated than usual. Staff at Boots the Chemist were instructed to explain that their eau de cologne did not come from Cologne itself, but was made in Britain and 'is, quite apart from patriotic reasons, preferred by the discerning'. Adverts sprang up in the newspapers promoting the importance of using British products and from naturalised shopkeepers with German sounding names assuring their customers of their loyalty. Elsewhere, the Lyons company sued rivals Liptons for spreading rumours that their board of directors were German, while the makers of Bovril rather smugly reported that they had 'always been British' and, consequently, had not needed to make any changes to the company's constitution or directorate since the outbreak of war, insisting Bovril was 'BRITISH TO THE BACKBONE'. In Harrogate, there was debate about whether the playing of German music to users of their Turkish baths should continue and, across the country, committees discussed the changing of any street or building names with German connections. Businesses dismissed employees with German roots while golf clubs withdrew memberships from long-standing members. The presence of a German nanny, a pre-war symbol of success for the middle classes, now risked the family being labelled as enemy sympathisers. The owners of dachshunds sometimes found themselves the target of mobs and their dogs killed because of their association with Germany, although, oddly, mobs tended not to attack German shepherd dogs capable of fighting back and instead settled for renaming them 'Alsatians' after the disputed French province of Alsace. For years, industrial centres like Bradford and Sheffield had enjoyed close links with Germany and there had been fears that Bradford's economy in particular was so closely linked to the export trade that war with its greatest customer would bankrupt the city – a fear only allayed by the sudden influx of orders for woollen uniforms for the British Army which, ironically, were dyed using chemicals previously imported from Germany.

Meanwhile, German chemical manufacture had turned from khaki dye to something far more deadly. On 22 April 1915, in a sector north-east of Ypres manned by Canadian and French Algerian troops, the glorious spring day was interrupted at about 5pm by an intense artillery barrage coming from the German lines. Among the usual clouds of white and black smoke that accompanied every shell burst, sentries noticed a greenish yellow cloud drifting towards Allied lines. In a little over ten minutes, 150 tons of chlorine gas had been released. Men began choking and brought up a thin, yellow frothy liquid, and panic spread. The Algerians, subjected to the brunt of the attack, broke and fled. The Canadians desperately used anything to hand such as socks, handkerchiefs and field dressings to try to cover their faces. Some broke bottles and filled them with earth or charcoal in an attempt to filter out the gas. An estimated 150 casualties reached the Canadian Field Ambulance unit that night, a further 885 the following day and, by 25 April, over 1,200 men had been admitted suffering the effects of gas. It was not only the front line troops who were affected. Sir Wilmott Herringham, a medical officer at a nearby Casualty Clearing Station recorded:

> *It was on April 23rd that Bowlby and I were at Vlamertinghe at the Canadian Field Ambulance and whilst in the dressing room in was brought a man whose clothes had a curious smell. He was wounded in the leg so they took off his clothes. In three or four minutes no one could stay in the room as everyone's eyes were watering badly although the man had been lying out for four hours on a windy day.*

Writing to his brother in Malton, Canadian soldier David Glenday reported that the gas had affected his face and eyes and that 'I smelt so bad of gas that they could not dress me. It choked the doctor. The General ordered my clothes to be cut off and given to him to be analysed … The sisters complained of the smell and in the hospital train they wondered what it was until I told them.'

Behind the front lines, Castleford man Private Ryans was serving in 'B' Company of the 1st York and Lancaster Regiment. He wrote home to Dr George Hillman of North View:

> *The Germans in their attempt to break through our lines used first of all on the French trenches asphyxiating bombs, causing the Algerians, who were in possession, to leave them. The Canadians, who were near, at once stepped into the breach. Our regiment was sent to help the Canadians, along with other troops. When we commenced to advance we were met with such a combination of artillery, machine gun and rifle fire that we were obliged to take cover for the best part of the day ... We got*

Artist's impression of the first gas attack near Ypres, April 1915.

the order to charge, and had at least 1,500 yards to go across
country in the face of the most terrific fire from all arms of the
Germans, who were lining the high ground to our front and our
right front. It seemed almost impossible that any of us would
ever arrive at our objective, but some of us did …

The actions of the York and Lancasters stabilised the front and prevented the Germans from taking advantage of the breach in the line, but the use of poison gas angered British troops. 'I think it is high time, and I am not alone in thinking,' wrote Ryans, 'that we took the gloves off to these Germans. They are out to win by fair means or foul. They have broken every convention and I think if the French invention is any good it ought to be used. The Germans would not hesitate if they knew the secret. If the people who object to the use of it could see half of what we have seen they would have no scruples, but would use any means to crush Prussian force. Milk and watery ways are not the method to beat a bully, especially when he happens to be a powerful one.'

The 'French invention' referred to was a new type of even more deadly gas being developed by the Allies. As early as 1914, French troops had been using tear-gas grenades and, like the British, secretly working on their own methods of using poison-gas to break the trench stalemate. The Germans, by making first use of it, allowed the Allies to respond in kind within weeks. As one British commander put it:

> *It is a cowardly form of warfare which does not commend itself to me or other English soldiers ... We cannot win this war unless we kill or incapacitate more of our enemies than they do of us, and if this can only be done by our copying the enemy in his choice of weapons we must not refuse to do so.*

A new and terrifying type of warfare had been unleashed.

Back in Britain, news of the use of gas was greeted with shock but not surprise. By now the image of the barbarous Hun was well established and few things seemed beneath them after the rape of Belgium. Then, on 1 May 1915, RMS *Lusitania* set out from New York for a voyage to Liverpool and, despite warnings from the German Embassy in the United States published in over fifty American newspapers alongside adverts for the crossing:

> *NOTICE! TRAVELLERS intending to embark on the Atlantic voyage are reminded that a state of war exists between Germany and her allies and Great Britain and her allies; that the zone of war includes the waters adjacent to the British Isles; that, in accordance with formal notice given by the Imperial German Government, vessels flying the flag of Great Britain, or any of*

her allies, are liable to destruction in those waters and that travellers sailing in the war zone on the ships of Great Britain or her allies do so at their own risk. IMPERIAL GERMAN EMBASSY Washington, D.C., 22 April 1915.

The *Lusitania* had been built using government subsidies with the proviso that in the event of war she could be converted for use as an armed merchant cruiser with her plans including readymade compartments for carrying arms and ammunition. When war was declared, she was duly requisitioned and listed in the 1914 edition of *Jane's All the World's Fighting Ships* as an auxiliary cruiser and, therefore, officially, a British war ship. As she made ready to sail from New York, her ship's manifest openly listed over 4 million rounds of ammunition and 50 tonnes of explosives on board. It would be her 202nd crossing of the Atlantic and she sailed with 1,266 passengers and 696 crew aboard.

On the afternoon of 7 May, the *Lusitania* was nearing the end of her voyage and expected to reach Liverpool that evening when she sailed into the path of the German submarine *U-20* about 10 miles off the coast of southern Ireland. In accordance with the warning issued in the United States, the U-Boat captain ordered his crew to engage what he had identified as an officially designated British auxiliary cruiser. A single torpedo struck her on the starboard bow just below the wheelhouse, but that torpedo's explosion triggered another, this time of the ammunition stored on board. Because of the speed and angle at which the ship sank, only six of her forty-eight lifeboats could be launched and 1,191 passengers and crew died. HMS *Juno*, a British warship, was only about an hour away, but was ordered not to go to her assistance and many of the deaths were caused by hypothermia as the victims awaited rescue. Irish civilian boats raced to the scene and began picking up survivors, but it was soon clear that there had been a terrible loss of life, including many neutral American citizens.

Immediately, the British press picked up the story as yet another German war crime, coming just two weeks after the use of gas against Allied soldiers. Fuelled by unsubstantiated stories leaked from the government about German children being given a day off school to celebrate the sinking, the papers were filled with condemnations of the attack with the writer Rudyard Kipling declaring that there were 'only two divisions of mankind today: Human Beings and Germans'. Britain needed the United States to support its war effort and ideally to join the war on the Allied side, so much was made of the deaths of American citizens, but the American public, many of them of German extraction, were not yet ready to support a war in Europe, and President Wilson failed to gain the support he needed to openly support the Allied cause.

In Britain, the sinking of the *Lusitania* was the final straw. The atrocity stories that had come out of Belgium at the start of the war, the attack on Scarborough and the east coast in December, the bombing of Great Yarmouth by Zeppelin in January and the use of poison gas the previous month had all created in the public eye an image of the Germans as barbaric Huns who no longer deserved to be treated as human beings. The king set the example when he ordered that all German royalty – including his own cousin, the Duke of Cumberland – be struck off the Roll of Knights of the Garter. Top-hatted stockbrokers expelled any German traders at the Baltic Exchange and the Stock Exchange before marching on parliament to demand the internment of all Germans in Britain, and similar action was taken by traders at Smithfield Market and Covent Garden. Golf clubs expelled members of German origin and workers at companies around the country refused to continue to work with men they had known for years because of their German names.

Things quickly turned violent. Anti-German riots broke out in the *Lusitania*'s home port of Liverpool, and in London where anti-immigrant tensions had been building long before the war. Soon, rioting spread to other areas. In Goldthorpe, shots were fired by a British shopkeeper as looters attempted to storm his shop under cover of an attack on his German neighbour. The case made headlines as the rioters appeared in court and the judge announced that firing into a mob and killing rioters was a bad idea, but that those hit should not have been there in the first place. The shopkeeper walked free from court while the rioters were punished.

In the wake of the sinking of the Lusitania *a wave of anti-German rioting broke out across the country.*

Among the survivors of the *Lusitania* sinking was Jacob 'Jake' Chadwick, one-time billiard marker at George Nelson's Billiard Rooms in Church Street, Castleford. Visiting friends in the town soon after the sinking, Jake explained how he had been sailing on his third crossing as a fireman in the ship's engine room and had just gone off duty when the ship was hit. At the time he was preparing for a bath when he heard the first explosion. Hurrying up onto the deck, he joined the crew in trying to launch lifeboats, but the ship began listing so quickly that few could be launched in time. As the ship went down, he explained how he ran along a thick rope before diving into the sea, where he took a lifebelt from a dead man and floated in a sea of corpses for two hours before being rescued.

The reaction to the sinking was at first muted in the Pontefract area, but a week after the sinking, rumours of what the papers called 'rough work in respect of German tradesmen' began to spread. In particular, George Stoser's home and butcher's shop at 1 Market Place and a shop in Shoe Market managed by a Mr Shirley were said to be the intended targets of an attack. Police under Superintendent Aykroyd moved into action on Thursday and Friday evenings to keep the gathering crowds moving, advising the shops to close at 8.30pm, and they remained closed for the next few days. A few threats were shouted but nothing serious took place other than a bottle thrown at the Shoe Market shop on Sunday evening. The local paper later reported that both Stoser and Shirley would be 'interned in due course'. In Castleford, though, things were very different.

It began at about 9.30pm on Saturday, 15 May at the top of Carlton Street, when a crowd started to gather outside a shop belonging to Charles Farber. Farber had lived in the town for twenty-five years and had become a naturalised citizen in 1900, but the crowd were in no mood to acknowledge the fact. The sharp rise in prices at the beginning of the war had hit families hard and many blamed what they assumed were profiteering shopkeepers for the spiralling costs. This was the perfect opportunity to get their own back. Reports claimed that the first stone was thrown by a woman in the crowd but, however it started, soon Farber's shop and home was under attack as the crowd – armed with 'an amazing supply of "ammunition"' spread up Welbeck Street. Stray shots hit neighbouring businesses, smashing the windows of

Charles Farber's shop on Carlton Street, target for anti-German rioting in May 1915.

Alexander Stein's former shop in Carlton Street.

Howard Naylor and Mason & Co as well as every window in the Farber family home.

At about 10.30pm, it was the turn of Alexander Stein's shop at 16 Carlton Street. Stein's nephews were serving in the British Army and he had been a naturalised British citizen for twenty-five of the thirty years he had been a resident in the town. Next came attacks on Charles Schumm's property and George Holch's shop on Bridge Street. Schumm, resident in Britain for forty-two years, had been briefly interned but released due to being over military age and because he was in the process of naturalisation. As the violence spread, the missiles became more erratic, with some aimed at the police smashing the windows of the Co-op and others hitting shops belonging to Alfred Wilson, Goodall's butchers and Barratt's confectioners. Around midnight, lights outside Baldwins were smashed to make it harder to spot the looters as Christian Bregenzer's property in Albion Street was targeted, followed closely by a fifteen-minute assault on Charles Karle's pork butchers in Beancroft Road. Karle had been a naturalised Briton since the age of 6. Throughout the riot there was, according to reports, 'a strong disposition toward looting', but unlike in other areas there was very little actually reported stolen. After a couple of officers received minor injuries, the police responded in such a way that, according to the local paper, 'there are no doubts persons with cause to remember the baton charges' used to clear the road around Karle's and into Temple Street. By around 1.30am, the town was quiet and, apart from an incident on Sunday night when a bottle was thrown through the window of the White Hart Hotel, the rioting was over.

The £2,000-or-so damage ('which will have to be paid out of the rates') in Castleford pales into insignificance when compared to the estimated £40,000 costs of events in Liverpool alone, and other major outbreaks had taken place in London, Southampton, Bradford, Nottingham, Sheffield and Cardiff, and there were even reports of disturbances in Johannesburg. Smaller incidents had taken place in almost every large town in Britain with over 100 police officers receiving minor injuries and at least one man, naturalised butcher Frederick Zohn of Bermondsey in London, driven to suicide by the repeated attacks on his business. In the aftermath came a national sense of embarrassment at the 'regrettable manifestations', and courts dealt severely with looters, describing their actions as the very opposite of patriotic and likening them to the sort of behaviour that might be expected of the Huns, but not the British.

The sinking of the *Lusitania* didn't just anger people at home. The Territorials of the 1/5th KOYLI had arrived in France in April and were still adjusting to life in the trenches. Private T. Witham, from Green Hammerton between York and Wetherby, was serving with Castleford based 'C' Company and wrote:

We are all very bitter after hearing of the Germans' latest piece of warfare, that of sinking the Lusitania. *It makes our blood boil, and we feel as if it would be a treat if they would come and meet us midway, both sides without their firearms and have a real honest set-to. Their methods make one think at times that it would be better if we were allowed to pay them back in their own coin. The war would soon be over and, moreover, we should have less casualties.*

The KOYLI cap badge had meant the Territorials had arrived to a heroes' welcome in Doulieu, a village that had been fought over earlier by the 2nd Battalion and where German soldiers had executed eleven civilians as a reprisal when a German officer had allegedly been shot by a local. There the battalion slowly began its introduction to the trenches under the supervision of the men of the 2nd Lincolnshire Regiment. For many, the first trip to the front was an anti-climax. Both sides stayed under cover and there was little to see from the trenches during daytime and only at night did no-man's-land become busy as both sides sent out patrols and working parties to check the barbed wire.

Sergeant Herbert Henson was in charge of two machine-guns and in his first letter home from the front he described the scene in their sector:

They call them trenches but they are more like forts it consists of sandbags making a parapet 6' high above the level of the ground and behind are the dugouts. The dugouts are like a little colony of huts they consist of earthwork and sandbags about 3' high with a roof of corrugated iron on top and earth ... We had four gun emplacements about 100 yards apart or so covered over from areoplane [sic] observation they were quite alright ... We have six men per gun and out of that we had to provide a sentry through the daytime and night time two men on duty and one sentry. I have had about a couple of hours sleep each night and get the rest during the daytime when I got the chance ... We mount the gun nearly on the parapet when it gets dark and keep a sharp look out for working parties and then you let them have it and by Jove they don't half cuss and shout.

Most letters home were cheerful and confident, like Private 'Norrie' Thurlwell's in early May to tell his parents that 'we are all as happy as can be and are making the best of everything'. But some showed an alarming lack of concern for a family's peace of mind. One such was that published in the *Doncaster Chronicle* from Private Whitham of South Elmsall, who told of what happened when a German shell landed nearby:

It blew two of the men clean out of the dug-out last night and over the parapet. It was a shocking sight to see for the two men were cut to pieces. The other two died a short time after and the Sgt was seriously injured.' [This would probably have been Sergeant R. Barnes of the Featherstone Company.]

Private Alfred Walters of South Kirkby wrote from his hospital bed to tell his family of his first battle on Whit Monday. It had begun with a massive bombardment and 'according to our airmen [the enemy] had sustained thousands of killed'. After seeing the Germans 'blown into the air', Walters and his comrades in the reserve trenches:

Opened fire on them with rifles and machine guns but the reinforcements they assembled were so considerable that we could only advance about 200 yards. They opened fire on us with their big guns and with ours and theirs going together, the noise was dreadful. In the trench next to me four of my pals were blown to bits. Just after that six more were killed and after that I don't know how many for it was my turn next. I got a bullet in the neck and it came out of my back. Mr Robinson was the first to attend to me but I had the wound dressed four times during the night so that I went through considerable pain. Later I had to be inoculated as a preventative against poison. I consider that I am lucky to be alive after what I saw on Whit-Monday night. In one of the hospitals near the firing line I saw some wounded Germans about 18 years of age. They had eyes blown out and legs and arms blown off.

Another observer of the action, Sergeant Seth Dunning of Tanshelf also described his experience in a letter home:

At Whitsuntide we were under shell fire for three days and nights. But I can tell you these Huns can fight. Our line of trenches was 200 yards from theirs and the 1/4th KOYLI were ordered to dig themselves in 100 yards nearer and some of our lads went before them as bomb throwers. When the Germans saw what was going on they made a scrap of it and they won, but our lads joined with the 1/4th KOYLI and fetched them out with the bayonet. We had some casualties but their losses must have been fearful, for our guns simply ploughed their trenches up. We are holding on to what we have got. It will be a Godsend when we are relieved, as we have been six days here and could sleep on a clothes line.

In June came news that Sergeant Major John Moore, 'well known cricketer and Wesleyan preacher', whose account of the fighting the previous October had been published in the papers the previous December, was dead. He had been training men on the use of hand grenades when he realised that the one in his hand had been triggered and exploded before he could get rid of it. At first his family were told he was likely to recover but he later died in hospital of his injuries leaving a widow and two young daughters in Halfpenny Lane. Similar stories began to appear more and more often. Peter Jones of Gillygate had joined the army at the age of 11 and served fourteen years in the Northumberland Fusiliers before leaving the forces. At the start of the war he rejoined and in June was reported missing, believed killed. He was 29.

In July, Harold W. Clark from Castleford described his day [all sic]:

ONE DAY'S LIFE IN THE TRENCHES
It was one of those sharpe crisp morning's in July, when the birds were singing their best. This morning however turned out to be a very Hot day still the birds would fly around as much as to say never mind boy's we will be happy, and still there were guns Howling as the shells they came over whistling that awful tune distruction. This was the day that our loyal comrades on our left known as the 5th York and Lancs (5th Y&L) belonging to 49th West Riding Division, it was here alas when their looses were great the German artillery distroyed life as easily as you would throw a burnt match to the ground, to the dismay of all, was [there], the Germans have taken the Y&L Trenches but not for long, reserves who were in the reserve Billets came along, through the reserve trenches across the pontoon Bridges & on to the Yser canal banks the reserves consisted of the 4th KOYLI and the 4th York and Lancs ready to do or die all fear had by now left the boys, one disire now was to retake at all cost. This did not last long the Trenches and dugouts were destroyed, our only gain was our firm position of the line we nearly lost, all arround was the dead, dying & wounded, some beyond Recognition. The Germans were buried as kindly as our own were laid to rest, It so Happened that this day of hell played with human life as if it were a piece of coal burning on your fires at home, this day was my last on the Yser cannal it was here I received my wound in the leg, it was just like a pin prick, caused by a piece of shrapnel as big as your hand, which dug into the ground, to my amazement my Captain who was by my side being Captain J.W.Walker He spoke to me saying whats wrong Nobby.

I said I Have been Hit sir, He said where but it wanted no looking for, where the shrapnel Hit me it had ripped my trouser's open the Captain took me into his dugout, and put his great coat under my leg so as to ease the blood from flowing so freely from the wound when someone shouted *** [indecipherable] killed. He went to Him saying as he went I will get you some bandage and see to it your knee when I come back, whilst He was away, Leut Acthinson came into the Captains dugout, smilled and said what have you been doing I only smilled at him, because he said to me earlier in the day I should get hit before the day is out a few minutes passed on when I remarked sir, I should be better in my own dug out He replied all right if you think you can manage, I got up dazed never the less I got to my own little [place].

As the casualty lists from the Western Front grew, another place began to feature regularly. In January, the Russians appealed for assistance in their fight against the Ottoman Empire in Turkey. In an attempt to help the Russians, encourage Greece and Bulgaria (both formerly part of the Ottoman Empire) to join the Allied side, and to undermine Ottoman control in the Middle East, a plan was formulated to force a passage through the narrow Dardanelles. The aim was to capture Constantinople (modern-day Istanbul) using a naval force made up of ageing ships considered too vulnerable for use against the powerful modern German navy and a land assault by British, Australian, New Zealand and French troops via the Gallipoli peninsula in a knockout blow that would destroy the Ottomans. Edwin Asher, Arthur Howard and Robert Henry Smith had been among the local volunteers who had allowed themselves to be persuaded to join the Naval Division back in September, and at the end of April they had stormed ashore as infantrymen. By June all three were dead, Smith being killed on the day of his youngest child's funeral back home.

The landings were successful but the Turkish defenders proved more stubborn than expected and the Allies became bogged down in a trench stalemate to match that in France. In an attempt to break out, another landing was planned in August at Suvla Bay to be made by the Yorkshiremen of 11th Division. Seaman Jack Gearing was one of those

Trench life at Gallipoli. In the baking heat of August, British and Turkish troops fought disease and flies as much as each other.

tasked with transporting the men to Suvla and later recalled that his passengers were all New Army volunteers, 'mostly fresh from training and few had seen action, so every sailor was given two soldiers to look after. We gave them our hammocks, made sure they ate well and gave them our rum. You see, we knew that where they were going would be like Hell on earth, so we gave them all the love we could, because they were going to need it. There was all these feelings. That's why I admire the British, they take it and they're quiet.

As we approached Suvla Bay on the night of 6–7 August, it was the darkness before the dawn. I stood on the gangway which had been fitted over the stern to allow the troops to walk down into the motor lighters. As the soldiers followed each other down with their rifles one got hit by a sniper and screamed out. I told him to shut up and put up with the pain or he would frighten the rest – that was my first scream of war ... I did my best to cheer them up and encourage them. But most of the time, I was quiet because there wasn't much you could say in the face of all that horror. It was important that they had their own thoughts, they had to come to terms with it in their own way.

In a report prepared from hospital, Major William Boyd Shannon of the 6th Yorkshire Regiment explained what happened next:

We were taken up in Destroyers, or rather on Destroyers, as the men were packed like herrings on deck. We passed fairly close to Cape Helles end of Gallipoli, and could see all that was happening around Achi Baba. The run took 3 1/2 hours. We landed in the new type of lighter, which has a little bridge that lets down at the bow, worked by chains. They draw exceedingly little and ground very easily on the beach. I am not certain in how many they are meant to hold, but we packed three double Companies on one when we eventually moved to Gallipoli ... Company commanders were told that the move was coming that day. We had the usual parade at 5.45am. There was an officer's conference at 2.30 and maps were supplied us of Suvla Bay district, and the Colonel issued orders for the battalion's section. A, B & C. C[ompanies], under Major Roberts ... were to land at the beach south of the Salt Lake, proceed up the beach about 200 yards, and form line with flank platoons in fours, then wheel half left, which would bring us north east and attack the hill Lala Baba. The orders were, no loading [of rifles], bayonet only ... We marched out at quarter to four, and we loaded on two lighters which were towed by destroyers, the destroyers also being packed with troops. We were towed from the bow of the destroyer, steering ourselves. The lighter too has a little engine of its own which can do about six miles an hour. It was an exceedingly dark night, almost pitch black. As we neared the peninsula we travelled slower and slower, creeping along eventually. There were search-lights moving from the direction Achi Baba, two of them seemed to pick us up. We had been told by the Colonel that the Brigade was covering the landings, and the 6th Yorkshire was covering the Brigade, so that the Yorkshire Brigade in that respect had been honoured by selection. As we neared the shore under our own engines we were greeted with a burst of rifle fire ... On arriving at the base of Lala Baba I ordered a charge and ran up the hill. About three quarters of the way up we came upon a Turkish trench, very narrow and flush with the ground. We ran over this, and they fired into our rear, firing going on at this time from several directions. I shouted out that the Yorkshire Regiment was coming in order to avoid running into our own people. We ran on, and about twelve paces further on, so far as I can judge, came to another trench, which we also crossed. We were again fired into from the rear. I ordered the Company to jump back into the second trench and we got into this, which was so narrow that wherever you were you had to stop, it being quite impossible for one man to pass another, or even to walk up it, unless you moved sideways. Another difficulty was that if there were any wounded or dead men in the bottom of the trench it was impossible to avoid treading on them in passing. There was a little communication trench running from right to left behind me, and whenever I shouted an order, a Turk, who appeared to be in this trench, fired at me from a distance apparently five or ten yards. One of our men on my left was sitting on a prisoner, and there were four wounded or dead men just in the bottom of the trench near me. I chucked out several Turkish rifles, in case Turks were shamming, and took a clip from one of them, which I brought home as my sole trophy. I had some difficulty in getting anybody to fire down the communication trench in order to quiet the enterprising Turk who was endeavouring to pot me with great regularity, but eventually got him. We had at this time not picked up any of the remainder of the battalion, so far as I could ascertain. I therefore ordered another charge over the crest of the hill which was just in front of us. We ran on, shouting that the Yorkshires were coming ... I was hit by soft lead round bullet smashing the upper part of my left arm completely. I got one of the men there – Private J. Cole, 11873 Y. Company 8th Duke of Wellington's Regiment to put on my field dressing, and made him fix up a tourniquet with the handle of his entrenching instrument. There were no stretchers or ambulances working at this time, which was somewhere about 6a.m. on Saturday morning, so I thought I would make a push to get down to the beach before my strength went. I started to walk in with my right arm round his shoulders, he holding my left hand and the handle of the entrenching instrument ... Six hours in a dressing station, absolutely unsheltered from sun or shrapnel, where the medical officer of the Northumberland Fusiliers tied me up very successfully & a stretcher journey of about 3½ hours in the afternoon, 2½ hours in a row-boat on a stretcher, where I got wet to the skin in a tropical rainstorm, which left me a legacy of five inches of water in the stretcher, and arriving just too late to get on to the "Soudan" Hospital Ship, a further journey to the Valdavia brought me at about 6.45 p.m. on deck, where I arrived with a very healthy attack of ague amongst other ills.

And that is all I know personally about the attack of Lala Baba and the battle of Suvla Bay, both of which cost the 6th Battalion of the Yorkshire Regiment very heavily indeed, our only consolation being that we carried out the most difficult task assigned to us, unaided, and have not let down the reputation gained by the regiment gained in France.

The Yorkshire landings were chaotic even by the confused standards of the Gallipoli campaign. The maps issued were poor quality and in the darkness men became lost. Soon, the Yorkshiremen of 32 Brigade were scattered across a wide area, each battalion fighting its own battle. Nineteen-year-old Leeds-born Ernest Lye had missed the initial attack due to illness. He caught up with his mates of the Duke of Wellington's Regiment on the 9th:

We could see them in the distance, skirting the Salt Lake and, even though we were so far away, they appeared to be almost too tired to drag one foot after another. It was when we came up with them and could see their faces that we got the biggest shock of our lives. What terrible thing had put that indescribable look of horror in their eyes? They looked haunted with a memory of the sight of hell! With their faces dirty and unkempt, and with their clothes torn and ragged, I thought of them four days ago as they passed me as I stood by the doctor's tent, with their laughing faces and tin triangles. I looked for some of the familiar faces – Ernie Shaw, yes! He's there. Tommy Knott, no. Where's Tommy Knott? ''Killed.'' "Herbert Butterworth, and his pal Frank Boyes; have you seen them?" "Frank was wounded and Butterworth went back to help him, and we haven't seen them since". Where's Paddy Whitehouse? "Oh! Over there with Lance Corporal Hullah" and so on. There were twenty left of our platoon of sixty-one. Only two officers left in the whole battalion ... We had a roll call on the slope of York Hill [Lala Baba] and the sight will be pictured forever in my mind. I thought of a picture I had once seen, giving a similar incident in the Crimean War. The picture was good but the artist couldn't put into the picture the wild haunted look I saw in the eyes of my comrades as they answered their names, nor could he put on canvas the heart broken sobs as some man's name was called and not answered.

On the day Ernest caught up with his unit, 32-year-old Sergeant Alfred O'Leary from Pontefract was killed as the 6th York and Lancasters pushed inland, as was Edward Dudley, a talented vocalist who had worked at the Prince of Wales Pit before the war. Herbert Pickin of Regent Street Castleford died serving with the Royal Munster Fusiliers and the list went on.

As the Suvla Bay attack, too, stalled, Castleford-born Lieutenant Herbert Winn had already been ashore for some time attached to an Indian Army unit he described as 'a little stereotyped but more pleasant than I expected'. By August, he was a veteran of the strange life of men at Gallipoli. In September, he wrote home about his experiences:

We arrived a mile from the shore about 9pm, after dark had fallen. From here we got our first sight of the war. An intermittent rifle fire was being exchanged between the two opposing forces and some stray shots passed our heads as we stood on the deck watching the shore. The sound they made was very weird, resembling that made by a large insect.

Even getting ashore when there was no real opposition was a difficult job for the heavily laden troops attempting to clamber down into the boats waiting to take them ashore. Winn and a fellow officer had to stand in the boats to catch men as they tumbled over the last step down into the rocking lighters. After time in the front line trenches, his unit was brought back to the beach where temporary shelters had been dug into the hillsides. He was, he assured his family, very well and had had 'a pleasant time', with little or no work to do. 'Bullets and shrapnel whiz over our heads occasionally but don't do any harm. The firing is however incessant a little in front of us – shrapnel is busting, rifles cracking and machine-guns cackling.' Settling down into a routine with a monotonous diet of porridge, tinned fish, bully-beef and bacon for breakfast, curry and rice pudding for lunch and tinned meat and rice pudding for their evening meal, all eaten against a backdrop of deep blue seas and sun-drenched skies where aircraft droned overhead intent on bombing the other side, and where Allied and Turkish artillery fought artillery duels that from time to time killed men enjoying a swim off the beach. 'It is curious to think that you and most of the people I know in Castleford are living the same sort of life when I am in the midst of such strange conditions,' he wrote wistfully.

With troops at a standstill in France and Gallipoli, rare good news came of the exploits of William Lappin of the Pontefract Company of 1/5th KOYLI out in France, awarded the Distinguished Conduct Medal 'For conspicuous gallantry on 27 October 1915 on the Yser Canal'. As his medal citation explained:

At 9-20am he proceeded on his own initiative and unaccompanied, to make a reconnaissance of the enemy's trenches. He went over our parapet and crawled across about 100 yards of intervening space and under the German's barbed wire to their parapet. He looked through a small breach in their parapet and obtained valuable information as to the condition of the trenches and the strength in which they were held, and successfully returned with the desired intelligence. On the 29th October Corporal Lappin again went over the parapet in broad daylight and crawled to a Bulgarian flag fixed by the Germans [to the wheel of an old wagon] about 80 yards from our trenches and 30 yards from their own and brought it, with its nine foot pole, safely back to our trenches under a heavy rifle fire.

That news was followed by a report from Pontefract County Court who heard that in the wake of the *Lusitania* riots, George Schumm's family was reduced to living in two rooms, the rest having been condemned by the council, who had agreed to excuse him his rent. He had been unable to re-open his business because of threats that he would be

Artist's impression of William Lappin's DCM award winning action.

attacked again if he tried. Unfortunately, he owed rent to one of the other businesses attacked, that of George Holch, who, according to Schumm's solicitor Mr Woodhead, 'like a modern Shylock, demanded his full pound of flesh'. The court heard that following the riots there were no longer any pork butchers open for business in Castleford and that Schumm was already in serious debt. The matter was adjourned until repairs were made to his home.

Nellie Green, AKA Evie Carew, the showgirl whose romance with Rowland Winn was reported around the world.

After a year of bad news, newspapers around the world seized on an item in the *Daily Mirror* of 27 December announcing the fairytale story of the secret marriage in October of Nostell Priory's Rowland Winn to 'one of the most beautiful and charming chorus girls on the London stage', Evie Carew, and boasting that 'not even the bridegroom's nearest relatives were aware of the romance and will probably learn of it for the first time this morning'.

Rowland, serving with the Coldstream Guards, had obtained a special licence for them to marry at St Saviour's Church in Paddington, but the wedding was a near disaster. Firstly the best man, Captain Wentworth of the Royal Flying Corps, was planning to fly to London

Copy of the marriage certificate for Rowland Winn showing his new wife's real name of Nellie Green.

No.	When Married.	Name and Surname.	Age.	Condition.	Rank or Profession.	Residence at the time of Marriage.	Father's Name and Surname.	Rank or Profession of Father.
220	29th October 19/5	Rowland George Winn	22 years	Bachelor	Lieutenant Coldstream Guards	17 Hill Street Berkeley Square	Rowland Baron St Oswald	Peer of the Realm
		Nellie Greene	23 years	Spinster	—	62 Delaware Mansions W	Charles Greene	Gentleman

from his home defence base but was delayed and couldn't make it in time. Next, after waiting twenty-five minutes for the couple to arrive, the vicar decided they'd changed their minds. The couple, 'smiling and happy' arrived to find he had left a few minutes before. Fortunately, the vestry clerk was still there. He leapt into Rowland's car to search for someone to perform the ceremony and found the Reverend G.S. Clarke, who agreed to officiate. Despite the *Mirror*'s claims, the wedding was witnessed by Rowland's father ('Occupation: Peer of the Realm') and Evie – married under her real name of Nellie Green – was escorted by her father Charles, (Occupation: 'Gentleman'). In fact, Charles was a restaurant manager and her sister was married to a miner, making Nellie of a very different social class to her new husband. Such weddings were not unknown, indeed the year before Earl Cowley had married actress Mae Pickard and 1913 had seen no fewer than three peers, Lord Paget, the Duke of Leinster and Viscount Dunsford, marry showgirls – but Rowland was making a very big decision by taking her for his wife.

Shortly after Lord Victor Paget married Olive May, a damning article appeared in *The Throne*, the unofficial journal of the royal household, explaining the need for the aristocracy to 'Prevent Hereditary Peers from Debasing Their Blood'. According to the writer, 'the very existence of the lords as anything but a mockery and a laughing stock — is threatened by a development of recent years which every day grows to greater and more menacing proportions. We refer to the increasing number of unions between hereditary peers and ladies of inferior station — mésalliances which strike at the very heart of the whole reason d'etre of the House of Lords.'

On the one hand telling readers, 'we have nothing to say personally derogatory to any of these ladies. On the contrary, we congratulate them most heartily upon the enterprise and ability that has enabled them to rise above the status of life to which they were born.' It went on, 'that you cannot make a silk purse out of a sow's ear is a principle that has been admitted since the earliest times … Pure blood is always a most salient factor in the selection of leaders of men, and has been so recognized all through history. And in the case of hereditary peerages which entitle the holders to a seat in the House of Lords, it is not merely a valuable qualification, but the sole valid one. Therefore the peer who has sullied the blood of his family and of his descendants should be *ipso facto* debarred, him and his heirs, from sitting in the Lords.' In other words, Rowland was risking his entire future and bringing shame to his family by marrying his 'uncommonly beautiful' new wife. A ban on actresses at court meant his new wife could never accompany him to the formal royal events which he, as an officer in the Brigade of Guards would be expected to attend, and so he resigned his commission in order to join his friend Captain Wentworth in the Royal Flying Corps, completing his training and being promoted to captain by mid-1916.

Stories about the couple, even today, claim that the family only learned of the secret marriage when the *Daily Mirror* broke the story eight weeks later and the *Yorkshire Evening Post* of 28 December 1915 declared that the only witnesses had been the vicar and the vestry clerk. Given the party his father had thrown for him just a year earlier, Rowland could do no wrong. The couple's marriage certificate shows that Rowland's father, at least, attended the wedding and signed the certificate as a witness. Writing home from France, Rowland thanked his father, saying 'Eve' had told him that his parents had been 'extremely nice' to her while he was away and expressing his hopes that they would get to know her, as he did, as 'the most loveable person'. By the time Rowland completed his flight training, Eve was pregnant with the first of two sons and living in a London town house paid for by Lord and Lady St Oswald as a sign of their acceptance of their new daughter-in-law.

CHAPTER 3

The War Comes Home

Lord Kitchener's famous Your Country Needs You campaign had encouraged over a million men to enlist by January 1915, but even at the start of the war Britain was facing a combined German and Austrian force of around 7.5 million trained soldiers and the two countries would mobilise almost 19 million men during the next four years. Against such odds the British could barely replace their own casualties, let alone hope to become strong enough to go on the offensive and try to break through the enemy lines. Not only did Britain have to fight in France and Belgium, but it also needed to maintain order in India, where tribal wars threatened the security of the British presence there. British bases in Singapore and Hong Kong needed garrisons. Thousands of men were needed to fight German forces in West and East Africa. And Irish nationalists were still threatening open revolt.

In an attempt to compromise between voluntary enlistment and politically dangerous forced conscription, a scheme was developed under Lord Derby in which men would attest their willingness to serve but would not actually be called-up immediately. Instead, starting with single men first, they would be called-up in batches as and when needed. The scheme saw very few single men come forward, although the response from married men who believed they would not be taken was better. The failure of the Derby Scheme paved the way for those arguing full conscription was needed. Realising that voluntary recruitment was never going to provide enough manpower to cover all its needs and that the Derby Scheme had failed, the government saw no alternative but to increase numbers by the use of compulsory military service. In late 1915, every man, woman and child in the country was required to complete a registration card giving details of address, age and occupation. Those in work deemed vital to the war effort, such as miners, steelworkers, farmers and the like, were marked with a star denoting a 'Reserved Occupation'. These starred workers were exempt from call-up. Anyone else could be liable for some form of service and from March 1916 would be 'deemed to have enlisted'.

The debate about the need for conscription had been around for years, but opposition was so strong that it had previously been regarded as too controversial for any government to try to bring it in during peacetime. Even now Parliament was deeply divided, but recognised that because of signs of the imminent collapse of the morale of the French army, immediate action was essential and so, in March 1916, the Military Service Act was passed. The response was dramatic when over 200,000 demonstrated against it in Trafalgar Square, led by the No Conscription Fellowship, an organisation founded in 1915 to fight against just such a move. Under the Act, all single men aged between 18 and 41 would be eligible for call-up but exemptions could be made for the medically unfit, clergymen, teachers and certain classes of industrial worker. Uniquely among the European countries, and in response to pressure from the No Conscription Fellowship, Britain also allowed exemptions for Conscientious Objection for men who opposed fighting on moral grounds.

Since 1757, Quakers had been exempt from any requirement to serve in the militia for home defence in case of invasion and this had been allowed for in the Military Service Act. More difficult to manage, though, were other forms of conscientious objection. Some were men from strong religious backgrounds, others held political beliefs that saw the war as being run for the profit of big businesses, while some simply objected to any form of state control over their lives. The problem was that with some families having several members at the front and insisting that everyone should share the burden, the authorities had to make difficult decisions about who should be allowed to stay at home.

Local military service tribunals were set up to hear appeals for

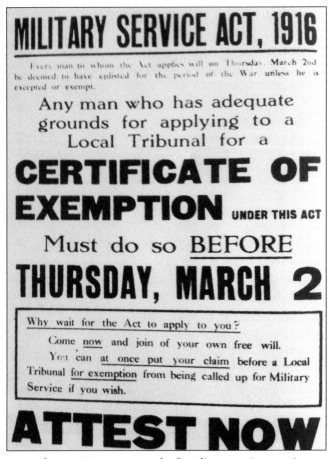

MILITARY SERVICE ACT, 1916

Every man to whom the Act applies will on Thursday, March 2nd be deemed to have enlisted for the period of the War unless he is excepted or exempt.

Any man who has adequate grounds for applying to a Local Tribunal for a

CERTIFICATE OF EXEMPTION UNDER THIS ACT

Must do so BEFORE

THURSDAY, MARCH 2

Why wait for the Act to apply to you?

Come now and join of your own free will.

You can at once put your claim before a Local Tribunal for exemption from being called up for Military Service if you wish.

ATTEST NOW

The coming of conscription saw a rush of applicants trying to gain some sort of exemption from military service. Some excuses were better than others.

exemption for all causes. Described as 'the sort of people you would ask to sign your passport application', they were local businessmen and traders, clergymen and even trade union officials, along with a military representative to present the army's point of view. Their job was to try to balance the personal circumstances of individuals against the national need. Often portrayed as heartless bureaucrats, theirs was an almost impossible job. A small trader might be put out of business if he were called-up but could, as some claimed, being the only person in the village who could cut hair, for example, really be described as work of national importance? So too tripe-dressers, hat-makers and corset-makers, all tried to gain exemption on the grounds that their work was far more important at home than fighting alongside their former neighbours and customers at the front. When 32-year-old Isaac Hayward appeared before Featherstone Tribunal, he explained he ran the Featherstone Main Cigarette Fund, sending an average of seventy-one parcels per week out to local soldiers. The tribunal heard he was a commission agent and asked, 'What does that mean?', to which his solicitor explained that Mr Hayward was a bookmaker and, since he explained, 'they have not stopped racing altogether', he believed he should be allowed to avoid service. The tribunal concluded that this was 'not work of national importance'. Of the first twenty-two appeals heard by Pontefract Tribunal, only five were rejected outright. Most were deferred to allow the applicant to either make alternative arrangements for managing his circumstances while he was away or to prepare a further appeal. Those refused exemption were legally regarded as having been enlisted and could be arrested by the military for failing to report.

Bert Brocklesby of Conisbrough, whose brother was already serving in France, was one of those who refused to report. He was arrested and taken to Pontefract Barracks and placed in the Guardroom:

> There were about thirty men in a room designed for fifteen. The stench of humanity and drunks was nothing to the crowning stench of a filthy latrine in the corner, of which the drain was choked and urine was seeping across the guardroom floor. I had to pick a dry patch. I did not feel happy, nor that I was suffering in a noble cause. I knew that these inconveniences were paltry compared with the sufferings brought to millions by the cursed war, but coming from an ideal home it was bad enough. Two blankets had been doled out, one for mattress and one for cover, but I had no pillow. I had brought my Teacher's Bible, which for many years had given light and strength. This served as a pillow.

The first category of conscientious objector, 'Non-combatants', were relatively easy for the Tribunals and military to manage as they were

'Conchies' were widely seen as hiding behind the freedoms that other men were prepared to fight for.

prepared to accept call-up into the army, but not to be trained to use weapons or indeed have anything to do with weapons at all. The British Army had no precedents or guidelines for managing conscription and so tried to compromise by creating the Non-Combatant Corps to provide a guarantee conscientious objectors (known as COs or Conchies) would not be asked to perform combat duties. Commanded by regular army officers and NCOs, they would be soldiers and subject to army discipline, but would not be expected to fight. Instead they would be a labour force doing a variety of jobs such as building, cleaning, loading and unloading stores other than munitions behind the lines in Britain and overseas. Around 3,400 COs accepted postings to the Corps during the war. Equally, 'Alternativists', who objected to military service but were prepared to undertake alternative civilian work not under any military control could be exempted on condition that they actually did this work. Alternativist James Digby, of Duke Street, Castleford, for example, was exempted combatant service in June 1916 and assigned to the Non-Combatant Corps, but was discharged the following March to work in the mines back in his home town.

Some, though, were 'Absolutists', who claimed to be opposed to conscription as well as war and who presented themselves as upholders of civil liberty and the freedom of the individual – values thought to be respected in Britain. Absolutists believed that any form of alternative service supported the war effort and in effect, supported the immoral practice of conscription as well. As a result, 'Absolutists' refused any form of compromise on the basis that working as a postman or tram driver could release another man for duty and therefore supported the war. In one case, a man refused to muck out horse stalls at an army remount centre in Britain on the basis that the horses were destined for service in the forces and by cleaning their stalls he would be 'directly contributing to the war'. The tribunals had the power to give these men complete and unconditional exemption but were reluctant to do so unless there was overwhelming evidence of their convictions. Ernest Luff of Ferrybridge Road was refused total exemption by Castleford Tribunal and ordered to report to the Non-Combatant Corps. He refused but was legally subject to military discipline and faced a court martial at Pontefract on 29 May 1916, and again at Richmond on 7 July, for failing to report for duty, and was sentenced to 112 days imprisonment. In Britain's pre-war all-volunteer army soldiers might be expected to accept its rules, even if they didn't always abide by them. But men snatched unwillingly from quite different occupations were another matter. Discipline had to be maintained and soldiers – even non-combatant ones – had to obey orders. For the military authorities, allowing men like Luff to pick and choose their own terms was an open invitation to mutiny by thousands of other soldiers. Luff, though, remained steadfast and a new tribunal held at Wormwood Scrubs later that year declared him a Class A conscientious objector. He was discharged from the army on 1 November. Others who, like Luff, found themselves in civilian prisons soon realised that their battle had not yet ended. Sent to Wakefield Prison, Bert Brocklesby recalled, 'I remember Father asking me what work I was prepared to do, if any. I said I would sew mailbags. He asked if that was not also war work as they would be used to carry letters for the soldiers. I said I saw no harm in soldiers having letters from home.' Others had a less charitable attitude and refused even this work, leading to further punishment. When the government attempted to set-up work camps as an alternative to prison, many absolutists argued that any work they might be asked to do – even peeling potatoes for use by anyone except themselves – would automatically benefit the war effort in some way and so chose to stay in prison.

At a time when conscription relied on men being willing to obey the law, allowing some to evade service would open the floodgates for all to claim to have grounds to object. Hundreds of young men moved to Ireland, where the political situation meant conscription wasn't being enforced. There were genuine objectors among them but also large numbers of men who simply did not want to serve. Some presented absolutists as being principled heroes and elaborate escape networks developed of safe houses willing to shelter men evading service, while others saw them as cowards hiding behind the freedoms other men were fighting and dying to protect. Some, like the man who refused all Salford Tribunal's attempts to grant him total exemption, were regarded as cranks; especially after he insisted that he must be exempted as a conscientious objector rather than because, as the tribunal's military representative pointed out, he only had one leg.

One of the first to appear before the local tribunal was 30-year-old scythe-stone-maker George Burton of Ackworth, who claimed absolute exemption in March 1916 but was granted non-combatant status. His appeal at Wakefield the following month was dismissed. Burton was assigned to the Non-Combatant Corps but refused orders and was brought before a court martial in May for refusing orders. At the end of the month he was posted to France, arriving there on the day Ernest Luff faced his own first court martial back home. Burton served there throughout the war but was again disciplined in December 1917, when he was sentenced to eighty days hard labour for refusing orders. Supporters of the COs wrote of men being 'crucified' for their beliefs, but while treatment of COs could be harsh, COs who were sent to non-combatant units and who refused to obey orders were treated the same as any other soldier, so when they consistently refused to obey orders they were usually given Field Punishment No. 1. Introduced in 1881 following the abolition of flogging, 'FP1' was a common means of dealing with military crimes overseas. A commanding officer could award field punishment for up to twenty-eight days or a court martial for up to ninety days, depending on the severity of the crime. Field Punishment No. 1 saw the convicted man placed in some sort of restraints and attached to a fixed object such as a gun wheel or a fence post for no more than two hours per day, three days out of every four. The punishment was often applied with the arms stretched out and the legs tied together, giving rise to the nickname 'crucifixion', and those who chose to see the COs as religious martyrs seized on the term. But one survivor, Alfred Evans, claimed that 'it was very uncomfortable, but certainly not humiliating', and in many cases conscientious objectors even saw FP1 as a badge of honour.

The issue of conscientious objection created a particular dilemma for the staff and former scholars of Ackworth School. Although it was one of eight schools established as a boarding school for Quaker children and run in accordance with Quaker beliefs, many of its students were not themselves Quakers and so had to make their own choice. Some old scholars turned to headmaster Frederick Andrews for guidance. Andrews was a prominent figure in the Society of Friends and had made no secret that he regarded war as 'the bankruptcy of

Christianity', but was proud of his former pupils who, he reported, were 'from conscientious motives undertaking National Service of a different character'. Andrews, though, would not condemn those who chose to serve, telling one old scholar that if 'a man has no conscientious convictions against war I honour him for enlisting'. Many felt his stance was a compromise of principles but Andrews was determined that all old scholars would feel supported in whatever they chose to do. At the end of the war he wrote of 'how my heart has warmed towards those who felt they must fight for justice – the rights of small nations, the sanctity of treaties, for Liberty and against militarism, how also I rejoiced in the spirit of the Good Samaritan so many Old Scholars gave themselves up to staunching the wounds and alleviating the miseries of war, and finally, how well I understood the

Former scholars of Ackworth School serving with the Quaker Friends Ambulance Unit, 1915. The coming of conscription meant a crisis of conscience for many men like these. (Courtesy of Ackworth School)

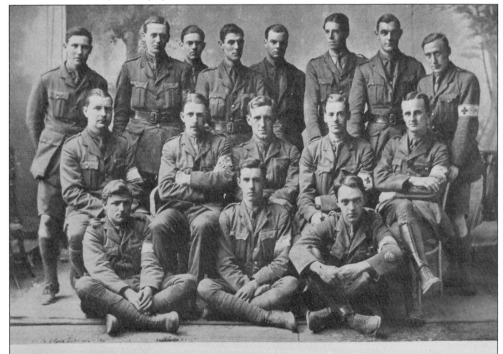

SOME OF THE OLD ACKWORTH SCHOLARS WORKING WITH THE FRIENDS' AMBULANCE UNIT, 1915.

F. G. Taylor,   C. E. Whiteley,   J. D. Dann,   H. H. Burtt,   S. Corder,   E. Cooper,   F. Tuke,   J. S. Carr,
S. Lithgow,   G. N. Hyde,   H. T. Brown,   H. A. Gilderdale,   E. W. Dunning,
E. R. Brady,   T. Burtt.   A. I. Messer.

OLD ACKWORTH SCHOLARS FALLEN IN THE WAR.

Former scholars at Ackworth School killed in the war. (Courtesy of Ackworth School)

Ackworth School's headmaster strove to support his students whether they chose to serve or resist. All were recorded with equal pride. (Courtesy of Ackworth School)

position of some of Quaker ancestry who felt impelled to suffer imprisonment rather than accept any form of military service. As their history shows they were no shirkers'. By the end of the war the school proudly reported having had 211 young men exempted from service, nineteen in prison, but 443 – including one colonel and three lieutenant-colonels – in the army and forty in the navy. Seventy had died.

At the beginning of the war some Quakers formed the Friends War Victims Relief Committee (FWVRC) and travelled overseas at their own expense to aid refugees forced away from their homes by the fighting, continuing the work throughout the war and its aftermath. At

*James Stout, in 1913 a member of the Ackworth
School cricket team. Two years later he would be
leading troops in France.*

the same time, another group of young
Quakers who were trained in first aid set up
the Friends Ambulance Unit (FAU),
explaining that their 'ideal as a voluntary unit
is to ease pressure on overworked or
inadequate staff'. Service with the FAU gave
them a way to help the wounded without
supporting the war itself, treating Allied and
German wounded alike, although as one member later explained, 'One
has to help the latter mostly by stealth, but it is lovely to be able to do
so now and then.' The French Army reportedly regarded the FAU as
'amiable and efficient cranks', but there is no doubt that their bravery
and determination saved many lives.

Of those former Ackworth pupils from Quaker backgrounds, 192
volunteered for work overseas either with the FAU or the FWVRC, but
the coming of conscription brought new dilemmas. Many conscientious
objectors given exemption on condition they served with the FAU

found their position increasingly problematic. Back in 1914, some FAU workers expressed their concern that they might be taking non-combatant work away from volunteer soldiers, meaning that men would be placed in danger and possibly killed because the FAU was doing work the soldiers would otherwise be doing. The coming of conscription meant that the men freed up for frontline service would not be volunteers who chose the army but potentially unwilling conscripts forced into the front line. Some, like Richard Evans, of 10 Carleton Terrace in Pontefract, were among those who thought that their exemption was unfair to other COs, whose hardships they felt they should be sharing. Evans served with the FAU from December 1915 to May 1916 but then resigned. He was lucky. Some who resigned found themselves confronted by tribunals who wanted to use their having been in France with the FAU as evidence that they did not object to alternative compulsory service and ordered them either back into the FAU or into the Non-Combatant Corps.

Those seeking to avoid service for any reason found little sympathy from men already at the front. Writing from France, Arthur Truman from Whitwood told the local paper: 'I believe there are a few left who ought to be doing their bit. It is not fair for one man to fight and another to get the spoils.' In hope of persuading some 'Carlton-street slackers' to enlist, Arthur turned to poetry:

> There are many graves in Flanders
> Where our soldiers lay at rest;
> Some of Castleford's band of heroes
> Who have done their level best.
> And their souls cry to their brothers
> Away across the sea –
> "Won't you do your duty also
> Under Lord Derby's scheme?'
>
> Oh you able bodied fellows,
> As your daily work you do,
> Can't you hear their voices calling
> "You are wanted out here too?"

Play the game and stop pretending,
Think of them in modest mien,
Emulate their noble action,
Keep their memories ever green.

Sleep in peace oh faithful brothers!
May your call be not in vain.
Though you sleep at rest in Flanders,
You have won a hero's name.

By the middle of 1916, those local soldiers who had enlisted at the start found themselves fully occupied with preparations for a major new offensive. A year earlier, the French commander-in-chief, General Joffre, had proposed that the Allied nations of France, Great Britain, Belgium, Italy, Serbia and Russia should co-ordinate their efforts in a more effective way and called for simultaneous large-scale attacks from all sides with maximum forces as soon as conditions were favourable in the New Year. On 20 January 1916, he told the newly appointed British commander General Douglas Haig that by the end of April he would have five offensives prepared. Three would be in the south-east, one in the Champagne region and one on the Oise-Somme Front, but which one would be selected as the main thrust would depend on the military situation at the time. Meanwhile, it would be important for the enemy to be pinned down and he requested that Haig attack north of the Somme on a large scale – a minimum 7-mile front – around mid-April 1916. The plan had no strategic goal other than to wear down the enemy as part of a war of attrition and so Haig said he could not agree. His forces (especially the untried troops of Kitchener's New Army) would not be ready, it would be politically unacceptable at home, and it would be regarded by the British public as a failed attack. After further discussion, Joffre agreed to change the plan, deciding that a combined Franco-British offensive should be carried out across the Somme some time that summer, with a smaller attack by the British in the area between La Bassee and Ypres. Haig, aware of the recent developments in the design of the tank, hoped to wait until August so that he could use them to maximum effect in the British part of the attack.

Unfortunately, on 21 February 1916, the Germans struck against the French at Verdun and it quickly became obvious that this was not a limited effort. The German commander, Falkenhayn, had declared an intention to 'bleed France white' by attacking the symbolically crucial forts at Verdun to draw the French Army into a battle whose sole purpose would be to allow the Germans to kill as many Frenchmen as possible. On 3 March, Joffre asked Haig to do all he could to divert German reserves away from the battle, if necessary by launching the Somme offensive early, and in turn Haig pressed the British Government for instructions about what they wanted him to do. On 7 April, despite his misgivings, Haig was told to prepare for British involvement in the Somme offensive. Britain was very much the junior partner in France, holding just 21 miles of the front with thirty-six British and two Canadian divisions, while France's ninety-five divisions held around 360 miles with every available unit committed to the defence of Verdun. It was difficult to argue against the French request for help.

On 29 May, Haig explained to the War Cabinet that in view of the small number of French and British divisions available for the offensive, far-reaching results should not be expected and they should expect something like 20,000 casualties. There would be no great breakthrough. The idea of a simultaneous Allied attack with maximum force was no longer a possibility, and the most that could be achieved would be to inflict enough damage on the Germans that they would have to pull back from their attacks at Verdun. Two days later, having been informed that Verdun was about to fall, Haig told his French colleagues that the British would be ready to play their part. On 3 June, he received orders from Joffre that he must attack at the end of the month.

Many of Haig's men were the untested Kitchener volunteers of the pals battalions, whose training had been improvised and with very few officers having any battle experience. This was a particular problem given the limited means of communication available to senior commanders. Radios were not yet advanced enough to be portable and the only way to get messages to and from a unit in the attack was by carrier pigeon or by a written message carried by runners. Both took time and meant that it was vitally important to keep men together so that platoons did not lose contact with each other.

The failure of the British offensive at Loos in 1915 had taught valuable lessons that had been incorporated into a manual published on 8 May 1916, which described using successive waves of troops to drive home the attack, reach the objective and have the ability to prepare captured ground against counter-attack (defences, for example, would need to be reversed and the layout of trenches turned around). To achieve this, and to avoid exhausting troops, eight waves, each about 100 yards apart, would attack so that the lead wave would only need to fight for a few minutes before fresh troops arrived to take over. Platoons would be divided up into different functions – some would do the fighting, some would 'mop-up' (clear the trenches of any remaining defenders after the main fighting). Others would be 'support' and 'carrying' units, bringing the tools, ammunition and heavy weapons needed to establish control of the newly captured trenches. While troops in carrying platoons might have to carry large amounts of kit, soldiers in the first waves would carry a rifle, bayonet, 170 rounds of ammunition, iron rations of bully beef and biscuits, two hand-grenades, a pick, shovel or entrenching tool, four empty sandbags, gas helmet, wire cutters and a water bottle. Although considerably lighter than the support platoon's load, this was still a burden and so orders were issued to advance at a steady pace so that men did not arrive at their objective too tired to fight. The order, though, was not set in stone. Brigade and even battalion commanders were able to make their own decisions about how their men would advance based on what they felt best suited the area they were operating in.

General Rawlinson, commanding the newly formed Fourth Army, was wary of asking too much of his raw troops and took a cautious view, looking only for small advances onto high ground and pauses to consolidate, ready for German counter-attacks:

We must remember that owing to a large expansion of our army and the heavy casualties in experienced officers, the officers and troops generally do not now possess that military knowledge arising from a long and high state of training which enables them to react instinctively and promptly on sound lines in unexpected situations. They have become accustomed to deliberate action based on detailed orders ... [They should] push forward at a steady pace in successive lines, each line adding impetus to the preceding line. Although a steady pace for assaulting troops is recommended, occasions may arise where the rapid advance of some lightly equipped men on some particular part of the enemy's defences may turn the scale.

Fourth Army Instructions 1916

The Castleford and Pontefract Territorials of 1/5th KOYLI were now part of 148th (3rd West Riding) Brigade of 49th Division, X Corps of Fifth Army, and preparing for their role as Corps Reserve. They would not take part in the first stage of the new offensive but were earmarked to push through any advances made by 32nd and 36th divisions in the area around Thiepval by crossing bridges across the River Ancre and quickly moving up to the fighting line soon after the attacks went in. Elsewhere, other locals prepared for their own roles scattered throughout the 100-plus battalions that would all take some part in the great attack. Over 1.5 million shells – more than two per second – had been fired into the German lines during the previous week and confidence was high among the Kitchener volunteers, although most admitted to a nervous excitement. At 7.30am, huge explosions rocked the German lines as tunnels packed with tons of explosives and dug by former miners attached to tunnelling companies of the Royal Engineers erupted to signal the start of the attack. Whistles blew and men began the advance.

In some places the attack went well. The King's Liverpool Regiment lost just two men killed, the Royal Warwickshires three and the Royal Welsh Fusiliers four. Around one in ten of the attacking battalions lost fewer than a dozen men as they pressed forward to their objectives. According to the War Diary of the 8th KOYLI: 'the first two waves leaving our trenches just before 7.30am, reached the German lines with only slight loss … The German wire offered no obstacle.' In some places, everything went according to plan. In others, the situation was very different.

Troops going 'over the lid'.

A wounded soldier is helped back to British lines under fire, Somme 1916.

British soldiers go 'over the top' on the first day of the Somme.

Contrary to the widely held image of the first day of the Battle of the Somme as being marked by lines of infantry walking slowly across no-man's-land towards uncut barbed wire and machine-gunfire, in many cases troops crept out as close as possible to the German lines before the barrage lifted so they were able to move quickly. Near the village of Serre, five 'saps' (small trenches) were dug along the 31st Division's front, each running from the British front line to within 30 or 40 yards of the German trenches. One hour before the assault, all the saps were to be opened up to allow troops to attack from cover. Once the attacking troops reached their objectives, two companies of the 12th Battalion KOYLI (Yorkshire Miner's Battalion) were to start expanding these saps into communication trenches, creating a trench across the last stretch of no-man's-land to the German line so that reinforcements could be brought up under cover. Two other companies were detailed to follow behind the Accrington Pals. As the divisional pioneers, the 12th had already completed one important task. Over the past few days they had dug mass graves behind the lines in readiness for the coming battle.

It was the New Army volunteers that suffered most. German artillery, already set to fire into no-man's-land and with their own trenches easily targeted, began to rain fire down on the advancing troops. German machine-gunners, protected by deep concrete bunkers, reacted quickly and began firing into pre-set overlapping zones of fire. Among the two companies of 12 KOYLI it was estimated that four out of five were wounded or killed. Their War Diary for this momentous day consists of just two sentences: 'Battalion reassembled at assembly posts at 4.30pm. Approximate casualty list 197 all ranks, including one officer killed and three wounded.' To their south, 8th KOYLI recorded that 'our battalion went into action with 25 officers, 1 M[edical] O[fficer] and 659 other ranks, of these the MO & 110 other ranks have reported to the Battalion'. Near Fricourt, over 300 men of the 10th West Yorkshire Regiment lay dead, the worst hit of all.

Not all those listed as casualties were dead. Some were lightly wounded and would return to their battalions within the next few days. Some were prisoners captured in German counter-attacks. Some were simply lost in the chaos of no-man's-land or the maze of the trench system and found their way back that night, but in the coming days and weeks, local newspapers would be filled with the names of the dead and missing. All around Pontefract families anxiously checked the casualty lists posted each day in the Town Hall and the papers. Tom Clegg, Percy Fox, Jim Higgins and Frank Terry had all gone forward with the 9th KOYLI in the attack on the village of Fricourt into 'a hail of Machine Gun and Rifle fire', followed by artillery and finally grenades hurled from the German trenches. All were dead. So too was Isaac Barnes, the Castleford miner temporarily blinded by the great storm of 1914. At Orvillier-la-Boiselle, John Fox, Lawrence Howard and Tom Mulligan were among the 8th Battalion's losses. John Bullock died alongside the men of the Leicestershire Regiment. Donald Leng of Hope Cottage in Pontefract had managed to fool the authorities into allowing him to serve overseas by adding a year to his age. He died with the East Yorkshires at the age of 18. Amos White had also lied about his age. At 44 he was over enlistment age when he joined-up. As a reminder that the war was still going on elsewhere on the Western Front, Wilfred Smith Turton of The Mount was killed near Ypres.

Over the coming weeks, at least twenty Pontefract families heard of the death of their loved ones that day, eight more in Castleford and another seven in Knottingley. More would die later of their wounds.

There were others, too, but not all home addresses were formally recorded by the Commonwealth War Graves Commission at the end of the war, so the true figure of local men who died on the Somme may never be known. Some appear on more than one memorial, others are forgotten altogether. Of the thirty-five men officially recorded as being from Castleford, Pontefract and Knottingley, twenty-two have no known grave.

The Territorials of the 1/5th KOYLI had been held in reserve during the first stage of the attack but the battle was not over yet. Parts of the German front line were now in British hands and it was time to maintain the pressure. On 5 July, they were ordered by Fourth Army HQ to attack and seize more German trenches to 'extend its two footings in the German front system'. According to their War Diary:

An unsuccessful attempt was made at 4am to seize more of the German 'A' system of trenches northwards towards the Ancre. The attack was made by 'A' company with 'B' company in support. The assault was met by heavy shrapnel fire and by snipers from various shell holes. Unfortunately all 'A' company officers became casualties ... The Germans thrice counter-attacked and twice obtained a footing in our trenches, but were promptly ejected.

Somehow the enemy had been alerted and the cost of this small operation was a heavy one, the leading platoons being almost annihilated. The fighting then degenerated into a series of attacks and counter-attacks with German stormtroops using 'egg' grenades that could be thrown for 50 yards to creep into the British trenches at night and toss their bombs into bunkers and dugouts. The KOYLI responded in kind. The battalion would continue to serve on the Somme until September, when news from the front was overtaken by action much closer to home.

By then, 20 million people at home had queued for hours to watch a seventy-seven minute documentary film shot between 26 June and 9 July by cameraman Geoffrey Malins showing the build-up and the attack of 1 July (although some of the footage, today widely used in documentaries as authentic images of troops going over the top, was actually staged at a training school behind the lines after the battle). *The Battle of the Somme* went on general release on 21 August to thirty-four cinema houses in London alone and would eventually be screened in eighteen countries. Playing to packed houses, the film attracted audiences who, according to *The Times* on 22 August, 'were interested and thrilled to have the realities of war brought so vividly before them, and if women had sometimes to shut their eyes to escape for a moment from the tragedy of the toll of battle which the film presents, opinion seems to be general that it was wise that the people at home should have this glimpse of what our soldiers are doing and daring and suffering in Picardy.'

At a pre-launch screening to military chiefs, Lieutenant-General Rawlinson, whose Fourth Army had suffered badly, felt that 'some of it is very good but it cut out many of the horrors in dead and wounded'. Even so, shocked audiences saw British casualties on screen and some walked out in protest. Across the industrial north, where women working in noisy mills learned to lip read from an early age, complaints were made about the language used by the soldiers in the silent film. Some picture houses refused to screen it, at Hammersmith a sign appeared reading: 'We are not showing the *Battle of the Somme*. This is a place of amusement, not a chamber of horrors.'

Pontefract man Alfred Firth had studied film-making in the United States before returning to set-up a cinema housed in a tent, which he took on tour around Ackworth, Cudworth and Castleford showing films like *Dante's Inferno* (1909), described as 'genteel pornography' with Virgil and Dante frequently portrayed against a sky full of floating naked women. Income was enough for him to establish an 850-seat cinema – The Playhouse – in 1916, just in time to screen the film and by October it had been booked by over 2,000 cinemas in Britain and even screened to troops in France, who generally seem to have approved of it. But if the film gave audiences at home some idea of what their men were experiencing in France, an even more graphic demonstration of the nature of modern war was on its way.

A year earlier, on the night of 6/7 June 1915, the L9, a Zeppelin airship, crossed the Yorkshire coast near Holderness and in just thirteen minutes unleashed bombs on the city of Hull that left twenty-four people dead and forty injured. There was anger in the city that there were no real defences against air attack and only a dummy wooden gun guarded by a single soldier mounted on the roof of the Rose, Down & Thompson munitions factory. Public fury spilled over into an attack on a Royal Flying Corps truck and stones thrown at an RFC officer in Beverley. In August, it was Goole's turn to be hit with bombs falling across the town and killing indiscriminately. In March 1916, Zeppelins returned to Hull and again in August. By comparison with what would come a quarter of a century later, these raids were minor, but their impact was enormous. Zeppelins were difficult to fly, could carry only small bomb-loads and, with air navigation in its infancy, they were frequently lost by the time they reached the English coast. Despite that, every alert created fear among the civilian population. Many fled into the countryside and production in factories stopped. Even pit winding gear was stopped whenever an alert was given and the Defence of the Realm Act had been strengthened to include flying kites and whistling for taxis – anything that might help guide the Zeppelins to their targets – but the fact was, the airships rarely knew where they really were. After raiding Sheffield, for example, the commander of one Zeppelin reported a successful attack on Lincoln, while his colleague that night, having bombed Bolton, reported having hit Derby. Such inaccuracy meant nothing. What mattered was that people on the ground began to believe that Zeppelins were the beginning of the end.

The biggest advantage they had was in being virtually invulnerable to British air defences. There were not enough anti-aircraft guns to defend every town in the country and the aircraft of the home defence squadrons, like those operating from Pontefract racecourse, were unable to climb high enough to intercept the airships which, by the time the rickety planes had gained enough height, were already many miles away and virtually invisible on a dark night. Even if they were able to catch one, it was only in 1916 that ammunition was developed that could both puncture the gas tanks and ignite the flammable hydrogen inside. It seemed at first that nothing could stop them until September 1916, when Lieutenant Leefe-Robinson became the first pilot to shoot down a Zeppelin over Britain and was instantly hailed as a national hero, winning the Victoria Cross and a cheque for £3,500, which he cashed quickly before new regulations forbidding such rewards were brought in.

A few weeks later, Zeppelin L31 appeared over London where it was spotted by Lieutenant Wulstan Joseph Tempest of 39 Squadron. Tempest was struggling with a fault in his aircraft that meant he needed to keep hand pumping a lever to maintain pressure in his fuel tanks as he flew towards the enemy. The situation was not helped by 'a very inferno' of anti-aircraft fire coming from London's defences buffeting his frail plane. Trying to keep pumping his fuel lever, fly the aircraft and fire his guns at the same time, Tempest closed in on the L31. 'I let her have another burst as I passed under her tail,' he later reported, 'and flying along underneath her pumped lead into her for all I was worth … As I was firing I noticed her begin to go red inside like an enormous Chinese lantern and then a flame shot out of the front of her and I realised she was on fire. She then shot up about 200 feet, paused, and came roaring down straight onto me before I had time to get out of the way. I nosedived for all I was worth with the Zepp tearing after me, and expected every minute to be engulfed in the flames. I put my machine into a spin and just managed to corkscrew out of the way as she shot past me roaring like a furnace.'

Known to the locals around his family home at The Grange in Ackworth as 'Billy', Wulstan was one of five brothers serving in the war. Eldest brother Alfred had already fought in the Boer War with the KOYLI and was now in the Canadian Mounted Infantry and Aelred – seemingly the black sheep of the family – had chosen to serve in the ranks as a sergeant, also in the Canadian forces. Wilfred was serving as a major in the 6th KOYLI after adventures in the Mercantile Marine, had twice been wounded during a stint as an officer of the Natal Mounted Police in South Africa, and had come back to England in 1914 with Wulstan and youngest brother Edmund so all three could join the 6th KOYLI together. Edmund transferred to the Royal Flying Corps in late 1915 and no doubt influenced Wulstan's decision to join after being wounded in the trenches at Ypres. Their proud father returned from a trip to Ireland when news of Wulstan's success was made public and arrived to find two telegrams: one from Leefe-Robinson congratulating him on Wulstan's award of the Distinguished Service Order, the other announcing the death in action of Wilfred.

Two successes, though, were not enough to deter the Zeppelin campaign. On Monday 27 November, Zeppelin LZ61, under the command of Kurt Frankenberg, crossed the coast over Atwick on Holderness as part of a nine-ship attack. As it headed inland, LZ61 drifted north. 'In all its long history', wrote the *Pontefract Express* later, 'the town which has borne the shocks and blows enough had not hitherto been the object of attention of these modern murder machines, the Zepp, although more than once like engines have passed over the old Borough elsewhere on wicked slaughter bent, so that Monday night's visitation was at once a novel and altogether alarming experience.'

Oberleutnant Kurt Frankenberg, commander of LZ61 during its raid on Pontefract in November 1916.

It began about 9.15pm when lamps across the borough dimmed as gas pressure was reduced – the standard warning of a possible attack. An hour later distant booms could be heard and locals assumed it was yet another raid on Goole or perhaps Leeds. Police 'Specials' reported for duty and people took shelter in their basements. Then, about 11pm, a series of loud explosions rocked the town. According to William Herbert Scott's *History of Leeds in the Great War*, the presence of a Zeppelin in the area that night, 'was made known by the sound of bombs dropped indiscriminately in Pontefract Park, twelve miles away, and the dull boom of the explosions was heard plainly on the north side of Leeds … It was, indeed, the flares which had been lit in Pontefract Park, to guide our aeroplanes there, that attracted so much attention in that particular neighbourhood.'

The newspaper claimed that: 'one or more of the terrible visitants hovered over the town and the neighbourhood for a considerable time, dealing out, had they been accurately aimed, sufficient bombs to destroy half the town and many of the dwellers therein, not to speak of

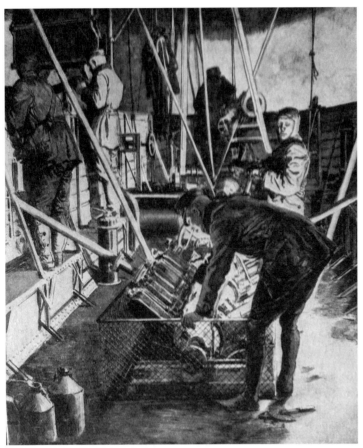

'Inside the cabin of frightfulness', an artist's impression of the bomb bay of a Zeppelin.

Commander and crew of a Zeppelin. At heights of over 15,000 feet over the North Sea, in winter Zeppelin missions often took up to twenty-four hours each. It was common to carry two crews as oxygen-starved men often passed out at their posts.

several big villages at some distance.' It was with a sense of disappointment that the report continued: 'In no instance was any damage of note done, no building was struck, and no person was seriously injured', although one 49-year-old woman with heart trouble had apparently died of shock when a bomb landed 300 yards from her home. In fact, it later admitted, only eight bombs had been dropped. Ignoring the possible danger, many rushed outside to watch as the airship passed overhead while others, the excitement over, went to bed. A few more distant booms were heard as the raid continued, when LZ61 meandered on over north Leeds, dropping bombs on empty fields around Harewood then turning south over Barnsley and bombing slag heaps near Silkstone. It then passed on, flying over the Potteries before heading for home. It never made it. LZ61 was attacked by British fighters over Norfolk and crashed into the North Sea.

The next day, thousands of people flocked to Pontefract to view the damage and hundreds carried away bomb splinters, broken glass or any other souvenirs they could find. With perhaps mixed feelings, it was reported that 'the prevailing feeling is of astonishment that the town should be worthy of attention'. On the following Thursday, an inquest was held into the only death of the raid in which the coroner concluded that her loss was 'directly due to the murderous barbarity of the enemy, that it was a disgusting and cruel shame. The jury unanimously returned the following verdict: – "Died from shock due to fright owing to bombs dropped by an enemy airship near her home."' Such was the shock of the raid that only 110 of the 270 pupils at Love Lane School attended the morning after the raid and it would be days before things returned to normal, popular belief at the time being that once a raid had taken place, it would be bombed again soon afterwards.

By late 1916, it was this new Home Front of Britain itself that had become increasingly crucial to the war effort. Both sides were fighting to defeat their enemy on the battlefield, but also to try to undermine his ability to fight. U-Boats sank British freighters carrying food supplies while the Royal Navy blockaded Germany to prevent imports getting through. Whichever side held out longest would win. To survive meant mobilising every available body to help and the pre-war prejudices about women's work had started to break down, albeit with the inevitable complaints of a decline in moral standards. In 1840, sensationalist newspaper reports described women working topless in coal mines and concluded it was a sign of immorality (an accusation that wasn't formally disproved until a report in 1911 showed women colliery workers to be no more depraved than anyone else). The loss of men to the war opened up new roles for women as drivers and mechanics, and especially in the munitions industry. For the first time, women were earning an independent income and the pay was enough that they even had money to spend on luxuries. Make-up sales soared and pubs noticed an increase in the numbers of young women enjoying a night out with friends. To combat the threat of yet another moral decline, special 'Women's Patrols' were set up around military bases to protect the innocent young women from debauched soldiery – or vice versa – by sending out patrols of formidable middle-class women who pounced on any young couple who looked like they may be enjoying each other's company a bit too much.

By 1918, up to 9,000 local women were reported to be working full-time in jobs previously reserved for men. For many, the huge munitions complex at Barnbow near Leeds offered good pay and daily free

Women surface workers load coal.

Munitionettes at work.

*Even before the war,
women were still
employed as surface
workers in some mines.*

Charabancs were provided to transport workers from outlying areas to huge munitions factories.

charabancs collected staff from villages around Pontefract, while others travelled there from as far away as York, Selby, Harrogate and Knaresborough on one of the thirty-eight 'Barnbow Special' trains per day needed to move the 16,000-strong workforce to and from their shifts, along with other regular scheduled services totalling sixty-four trains arriving there every twenty-four hours. The workers, drawn from over 130,000 applications, worked on eight-hour shifts from 6am to 2pm, 2pm to 10pm or 10pm to 6am, six days a week with one Saturday off every three weeks and without any holiday time. Typical munition workers' earnings for a full week averaged £3 0s 0d with skilled workers a possible £5, and even the girls who swept up waste for recycling could potentially earn up to £1 17s 0d. At one point wage costs reached £24,000 per week, but it was claimed that the cost of producing munitions at Barnbow compared favourably with any other similar factory in the country.

Three canteens were provided, each catering for up to 1,000 people at a sitting and a hot drinks buffet was provided for those taking their own food. Six young women tended a dairy herd of 120 cows producing 300 gallons of milk a day. Vacant land nearby was cultivated for crops producing 200 tons of potatoes in 1918. A slaughter house and butcher's shop supplied fresh meat from pigs fed on the ample amounts of kitchen waste from the canteens. Stables housed seventy ponies used for haulage work to pull loads to the 150 train trucks loaded every day in 1916, and this would rise to 600 truckloads by 1918.

But while wages in the armaments industry were good and jobs in demand, it was not easy work. The shells being manufactured were filled with 'Lyditte', an explosive made using picric acid, a yellow substance previously used in textile dyeing. Continued contact with it soon began to affect the workers as skin, eyes and hair all began to turn yellow, earning 'munitionettes' the nickname 'canaries'. Many made a joke of it but it could prove fatal as toxins built up in the body. Nor was it safe. Just after 10.00pm on Tuesday 5 December 1916, several hundred women and girls had just started their shift at the factory, 170 going to Room 42, where 4.5 inch shells were being filled, fused and prepared for delivery. At 10.27pm a violent explosion suddenly rocked the shed, killing thirty-five women outright, and maiming and injuring many more, leaving many of the dead only identifiable by the identity discs they wore around their necks. The machine where the explosion occurred was completely destroyed. Yet so vital was the work that production was stopped only for a short while, and once the bodies were removed, other girls volunteered to work in Room 42 that same night. When supervisor Arthur Peck arrived the next morning, he found: 'work was going on as normal but Room 42 was a bloodstained shambles. The accident is believed to have happened when a shell exploded as it was being fused, probably because it had been too tightly screwed down.' A simple mistake, easy to make for a distracted worker but with disastrous consequences. The youngest victim, Leeds-born Edith Sykes, was just 15 years old.

Wartime censorship meant there was no reporting of the incident in the papers but it was an open secret across Leeds, York, Harrogate and all the other towns and villages that had supplied workers to the site. An inquest was held at which 'only very formal evidence' was heard and it was concluded that there was no negligence involved. Over the coming weeks, claims were submitted to the Ministry of Munitions for compensation. Castleford's 39-year-old Eliza Grant had been killed leaving seven children aged 6 to 17, all now regarded as in 'partial dependency' of her income of 19s 6d per week, and so her family was awarded £65. Eighteen-year-old Mary Gibson of 93 Nicholson Street had contributed 21s 9d per week to support her father and five siblings. They were granted £90, as was the family of Polly Booth at 22 Rooks Terrace. By January 1917, claims for 22-year-old Edith Levitt of Navigation Road, Lock Lane, Helena Beckett of 33 Dunwell Terrace in Pontefract and Jennie Blackamore of Lower Station Road in Normanton were still being agreed. Secrecy meant that in most cases the victims received very little attention, their notices in the local papers

(8) Katherine Bainbridge. Age 30. Claimant: husband age 45 — a discharged soldier. 4 children 3 boys 10, 5 and 2, and girl 7. Claimant has a pension of £1 a week until June 1917 He states that deceased contributed 26/- weekly to support of household. Her average weekly wages is given as 17/5. Remarks: Partial Full dependency of children.

Compensation claims for local women killed in the Barnbow blast.

mother age 53. 4 children ages 24, 21, 15. 6.
28/2/17 Eldest girl contributes   17 : 0
         "   boy   " (soldier)   9. 2
         younger "   "   11. 0.
Deceased is said to have given her mother all her earnings £1 : 2 : 0 (avg)
Remarks Partial dependency case.
Is claimant a widow?

(6) Olive Yeates: age 17. Claimant father, age 43, Railway ticket collector earning 38/- a week One boy age 7 left. Deceased worked two weeks - average 11/6

noting only that they had died in accidents or 'in her country's service'. An exception was 20-year-old Jane Few of Newtown, Pontefract.

Jane, fifth daughter of William and Emily Handley had just turned 20. Only five weeks earlier she had married Charles Few, her pre-war fiancé who was on convalescent leave after being wounded in France where he was serving with the Royal Field Artillery. 'The deceased,' wrote the *Pontefract Express*, 'was a very able worker, and would have ceased the occupation on her marriage but for the fact that her services were valuable.' Her mother was too ill to attend the funeral but the family told the paper they 'did not find fault' with the efforts made to save her after the accident. 'We need not go into details as to the cause of death,' the paper continued, but said that, 'the funeral really became a demonstration of sympathy on a huge scale. There was a great concourse of people.' In March, one person had been killed and two injured in an explosion at Hickson's plant in Castleford, which was producing TNT and, perhaps in recognition of the feelings of many local people that such deaths were just as much part of the war as those at the front, Jane's photograph appeared in that week's column of local war dead.

Tribute to Jane Few, 1916.

As 1916 drew to a close, it seemed the war was coming ever closer to home.

CHAPTER 4

'For God's Sake Don't Send Me'

The third Christmas of the war was marked, like those before, by parcels of gifts sent from family, friends and well-wishers to those serving overseas. Local pubs and clubs had been collecting from patrons every week to ensure that old regulars were not forgotten by sending packages of cigarettes, tobacco or other little treats on a rota basis to as many men as possible, and at Christmas a special effort was made to provide a little something for everyone. In the coming weeks, thank you notes coming back showed the extent of the 'world war'.

Mr J. Schofield, landlord of the Aire Street Hotel in Knottingley, organised a collection for local men. By January, letters came back not just from France, but from across the world. Private A. Hutchinson was serving with the Northumberland Fusiliers in Salonica (modern day Thessaloniki in northern Greece) and told his old mates: 'I have been wounded in the arm but I am back now doing a bit more so I shall not get back home yet. I have met Crock Walker and Jack Bennet, tell Eli to write. I wish I was having a pint just now.' His friend Eli Cocker, serving with the East Yorkshire Regiment, had struck lucky. The 2/4th battalion had set sail in November and by January he wrote: 'Arrived alright at Bermuda and I thank you very much for the cigs. It is beautiful here, bananas, oranges, etc. Wishing you a happy New Year. Keep on smiling 'till the boys come home.'

Private Batty of the Royal Army Medical Corps was in Malta and found the parcel: 'a pleasant surprise – It is good to know we are remembered at home – I shall be pleased to see Knottingley again, I had not seen it for a considerable time until I came from hospital after recovering from a bullet wound received on the Somme.' Thirty-one year old former bottle-blower John Spence Hirst was with the 1/5th KOYLI: 'I am back here alright and in good spirits. All the lads send best respects and thank you for the cigs. I told them what a fine time I had with you all. Give my best respects to John Heatings, Billy Horton and Jack Hampshire.' Private Noble Wray, at the 39th General Hospital near Le Havre, wished everyone at home 'a bumping Christmas and a War-ending New Year', telling the lads that French beer was nothing like the stuff at home. He could, he claimed, 'sup it for a month without sleep'.

Cheery news and gossip from the front was always welcome, but for a time another battle between an Englishman and a German seized the public attention in May 1917 and brought Pontefract into the spotlight. Johann Wilhelm Gruban, a German-born businessman, had moved to England in 1893 to join engineering company Haigh and Company. By 1913 he had changed his name to John Gruban and become a partner in Haigh, Gruban & Co after managing to not only turn around the failing business but to make it into one of the leading manufacturers of the machine tools desperately needed by the munitions industry. Seeking to raise £5,000 funding to expand the business, Gruban was introduced to Pontefract's Liberal member of parliament, Frederick Handel Booth, who also happened to be chairman of the Yorkshire Iron and Coal Company. In 1912, Booth was part of the committee set up to investigate allegations of insider trading brought against senior Liberal figures including Lloyd George, who had bought 1,000 shares in the Marconi Company at £2 each before they went on public sale at £3.10s. The committee was widely viewed as a whitewash in which Booth had vocally supported his party seniors. As a result, he was thought to be held in high regard by Lloyd George and others and he told Gruban that he could do 'more for [your] company than any man in England'. Booth claimed close friendship with the then minister for munitions and future prime minister David

Lloyd George, Lloyd George's secretary Christopher Addison, and contacts with many other important government officials. Borrowing £3,500 from his brother-in-law, Booth immediately invested in Gruban's company.

In the wave of anti-German feeling that followed the sinking of the *Lusitania* Gruban's thick German accent meant he could hardly disguise his origins. Worried that he would find it difficult to get government work he again contacted Booth, who offered to help provided he was put on the board of directors of Haigh, Gruban & Co. If Gruban agreed, Booth promised he could 'do with the Ministry of Munitions what I like'. Over the next three months, Booth claimed £400 in expenses and complained it was not enough for the work he was doing, demanding he be given a secret payment of 10 per cent of the value of a new contract being negotiated worth around £6,000. Gruban refused and whilst outwardly continuing to appear supportive, Booth began to systematically undermine him.

Over the next few months a series of complaints came from the ministry of munitions about Gruban's work and his German origins. In November, a letter from "Lewis Ransome" reached Addison's office complaining that Gruban was a recently naturalised German: 'Although in normal times Messrs Haigh, Gruban & Co are competitors of my firm,' he wrote, 'I hope you will not misconstrue my motives in drawing this matter to your attention.' A junior aide had written in the margin that the complaint should be ignored but Addison himself intervened and in a written statement said it was 'undesirable that any person of recent German nationality or association should at the present time be connected in an important capacity with any company or firm engaged in the production of munitions of war'. Booth showed this to Gruban and, according to Sir Patrick Hastings, who later represented Gruban in court: 'he propounded what was practically an ultimatum. Mr Gruban, he said, was in the direst peril and there was only one means by which that danger could be averted. If Gruban would consent to hand over all his interest in his business to Handel Booth, who would, of course, hold it merely as a nominee, the authorities would be satisfied and Gruban would be safe. If not, his property would be forfeit and he himself would be incarcerated. In his desperation and in complete reliance on his friend, Gruban consented. Handel Booth became possessed of everything. Within a week Gruban was arrested and interned.' The arrest came after Booth had personally written to the ministry of munitions claiming that Gruban had 'taken leave of his senses', and the ministry ordered Gruban interned. Behaving like a pantomime villain, having taken Gruban's income from him, Booth refused to provide any support to the wife and family of the man who had thought him a friend and whose trust he had betrayed.

Gruban appealed against his internment and won his freedom, the judges recommending he seek legal advice about what to do about regaining control of his company. Two years to the day after the sinking of the *Lusitania* such huge crowds gathered in the Strand to hear news of the sensational case of a German daring to sue an English member of parliament that barristers struggled to get into the law courts.

Acting as counsel for Gruban, Sir Patrick Hastings was the first to speak and his opening speech criticised Booth for loving money rather than his country, saying that one of the things the English prided themselves on was fair play, 'no matter how loudly the defendant raises the cry of patriotism, I feel sure that your sense of fair play, gentlemen, will ensure a verdict that the defendant is unfit to sit in the House of Commons, as he has been guilty of fraud'. Gruban was called to the witness stand and asked to tell the jury what had happened. In a gamble, Hastings issued a subpoena to the prime minister and the home secretary in an attempt to discover whether Booth had written the letter that had led to Gruban being interned. He refused to proceed with the case until he had heard from one or other and, after a lengthy delay, Booth's lawyer handed over a copy of the letter.

Booth's testimony claimed that it was Gruban who had portrayed himself as a man of influence and that it was Gruban helping Booth, not the other way around. He went on to say that he would never have asked for a 10 per cent commission on the Birmingham contract, and that he had never claimed he could influence government ministers. Hastings produced the 'Birmingham Contract' memo in Booth's own handwriting and a telegram from Booth to Gruban in which Booth claimed that he had 'already spoken to a Cabinet Minister and high official' on Gruban's behalf. Addison distanced himself from Booth and told the court that 'to say that Gruban's only chance of escape from internment was to hand over his shares to Mr Booth was a lie'.

In his summing up the judge, Mr Justice Coleridge was 'on the whole unfavourable to Booth' but pointed out that Gruban's nationality might prejudice the jury. He need not have worried. 'Twelve Englishmen sat upon the jury,' wrote Sir Patrick Hastings, 'and they proved to me if ever it had been in doubt that justice as between man and man comes first in every English mind. Even an enemy gets justice in an English court.' It took the jury just ten minutes to agree that Booth was guilty and awarded Gruban almost £5,000 in damages. The following year Booth moved away from Pontefract and stood for election in Wentworth but failed to win a seat.

If Booth had brought shame to the district, it was quickly balanced by news of a Castleford hero. Thomas Bryan, a 35-year-old father of five, was born in Stourbridge, Worcestershire, but had moved with his parents to Castleford when he was very young and had played rugby for Castleford in the 1906–07 season until the club withdrew from the Northern Union because of financial problems. A miner by profession, Bryan left his home on Hunt Street in Castleford to enlist into the 25th (Service) Battalion (2nd Tyneside Irish) of the Northumberland Fusiliers in April 1915.

Thomas Bryan, Castleford's VC.

On 9 April 1917, the battalion was involved in fighting around Vimy Ridge, near Arras in northern France, when their advance was held up by a well-hidden German machine-gun. Among those killed was another local man, Fred Barber of Pontefract, whose sister Helena had died at Barnbow in December. Seeing his mates pinned down, Bryan decided to do something about it. Using shell-holes as cover, he crossed no-man's-land and entered a communications trench held by the enemy, surprising three German soldiers who promptly surrendered. Sending them back across to where his men were waiting, Bryan pressed on. Soon he was spotted and a burst of fire hit him in the right arm but he fired back and quickly realised that the crew were trying to get away. He fired again, killed them both and captured the gun. According to the citation for his Victoria Cross, 'He worked up most skilfully along a communication trench, approached the gun from behind, disabled it and killed two of the team as they were abandoning the gun. As this machine-gun had been a serious obstacle in the advance of the second objective, the results obtained by Lance Corporal Bryan's gallant action were very far-reaching.' The first Victoria Cross awarded to the Northumberland Fusiliers since the Indian Mutiny was awarded to Bryan by the king at a ceremony in St James' Park in Newcastle, where the reading of his citation was greeted with 'thunderous applause' from a crowd of 40,000 who had gathered for the occasion.

Back home, Castleford set about ensuring that 'Lance Corporal Thomas Bryan the Whitwood Mere soldier who so brilliantly won the Victoria Cross' received an appropriate welcome when he came home on leave. According to the *Pontefract and Castleford Express* of 22 June:

The king awards Thomas Bryan his medal in front of a crowd of 40,000 people.

A special meeting of Whitwood Urban Council was held on Monday night to consider what steps to take to celebrate the great event locally. The Chairman ... was particularly proud that it was one of the workmen of Messrs Briggs and Co who had won the V.C. They felt that he belonged to them. He was hoping that things like this would break down the barriers that existed in their common life and that they would get nearer to each other and appreciate each other has brothers. It might be that the world was in a state of pregnancy – that a new world was to be born, and England was at a very critical period in her history, not so much in the war but in the steps she would take afterwards. But for such men as Lance Corporal Bryan they would not be sitting round that table.

A resolution was passed to create a war honours fund to provide a gift of £20 to any local man who won a military award, and it was agreed that Bryan should be given a civic reception when he came home the following weekend.

A meeting of the reception committee was held at Whitwood Council Office on Wednesday night when it was reported that Lance Corporal Bryan would arrive at Castleford Station tomorrow (Saturday) at 3pm. Arrangements were made for him to be received by members of the Whitwood and Castleford Urban Councils, and for a procession to be formed to parade down Station Road, up Carleton Street, into Albion Street, along Wilson Street to Leeds Road and on to Hunt Street, where is the gallant soldiers home. Here there is to be a short halt for a little speech-making and then the procession will proceed to Lower Whitwood, rounding the shelter, and will return to the Cricket Field at Hightown, where there will be a public reception ... The Potteries generally, and Hunt Street in particular, have been decorated and beflagged throughout this week and there is everywhere evident determination to make the homecoming a red-letter day, not only in the life of the popular hero, but in the history of the Township.

Notices were posted around the town announcing that:

> *Lance Cpl. T. Bryan, V.C. will arrive at the NORTH EASTERN*
> *STATION, CASTLEFORD at 3pm Saturday June 23rd 1917 The*
> *PUBLIC generally are requested to show their APPRECIATION*
> *of his gallantry by a LIBERAL DISPLAY OF FLAGS AND*
> *BUNTING in the streets of the respective townships.*

That afternoon's *Yorkshire Evening Post* described how the Bryan family arrived home from Newcastle to find Castleford 'profusely decorated' with flags, banners and evergreens with every house on Hunt Street bedecked with flags. A small girl 'selected by the Hunt Street residents' presented Mrs Bryan with a bouquet of flowers before 'a triumphal procession comprising three brass bands, members of the Urban Council, friendly societies and school children in drays' paraded around the town and into Hunt Street behind the Bryan family, including his father, in a decorated landau. At a time when good news from France was rare, people made the most of their new hero.

Hunt Street, home of Castleford's VC hero, Thomas Bryan. In 1917, every house was hung with bunting and flags.

Elsewhere, further afield, 47-year-old John Burnill, of 170 Glebe Street in Castleford, sent long letters home to his father and daughter describing his experiences with the 'Mechanical Transport' *en route* to his camp from where, he said, he could sometimes see Mount Kilimanjaro 140 miles away. The journey had taken him via Durban in South Africa where 'the scene at night when the lamps were lit was like fairyland'. He wrote admiringly of the town's well-paved roads, claiming 'were it not for the surroundings you could imagine yourself in Leeds or any other Yorkshire town', although it may have taken a stretch for his family to compare Castleford in winter to South Africa in summer. A triumphant march through the town had seen the men showered with tobacco, books and cakes as the 'inhabitants vied with each other to bring gifts … it was a joy to be there and worth all the hardships undergone in the service'. From there he travelled to Nairobi and wrote to his daughter of the sights and sounds of Africa and life in 'one of the outlying outposts of our great and glorious empire'.

Even as John was enjoying life in East Africa and Eli was soaking up the sun in Bermuda, back home their families were struggling to cope with ever greater pressures. For the first time in living memory,

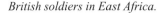

British soldiers in East Africa.

British soldier with mascot, Mesopotamia.

British homes were under direct attack and every man, woman and especially child had a role to play. Services like the police and post office frequently recruited ex-servicemen, many of whom were recalled in the first few days of war. With rumours of German spies everywhere, the authorities turned to youth organisations like the boy scouts for help. Scout patrols guarded 'vulnerable points' like railway bridges against sabotage, while sea scouts created coast-watching stations to look out for enemy shipping and earn the title 'Men of the Second

Line'. Shortly after war broke out, scouting district commissioner Frank Somner Hatchard of Stapleton Hall took out an advertisement announcing that: 'a number of handy and well trained Boy Scouts (ages 14-19) are available for outdoor or indoor work in this district only. Harvest hands, gardeners, clerks, messengers, cooks, typists &c. &C.' Followed soon afterwards by a more detailed ad explaining that there were scouts already in full-time work who were willing to do other jobs in their spare time, others were looking for paid work 'in order to be self-supporting', and a third group willing to help out their neighbours at home. Soon, scouts were helping refugees settle in, working as messengers and clerks at the barracks and in hospitals, helping bring in the harvests and acting as runners for the police, emergency services and the army. So important was their contribution that it became illegal to wear a scout uniform if you were not an active member of the movement. Scouts old enough to enlist (an estimated 10,000 in the first four months of the war) found that membership meant almost immediate promotion and some units, like one company of 240 men of the 5th Highland Light Infantry, were made up entirely of former scouts and scoutmasters. Other youth organisations also quickly rallied behind the war effort and children in schools began collecting on various flag days for causes as widespread as support for Serbia, comforts of troops and help for local men held prisoner in Germany.

The declaration of war in 1914 raised hopes that schools would close. Many did, taken over by the military as temporary barracks or as hospitals, but usually only as short-term measures. Love Lane Junior Mixed School, for example, was used to store military supplies and the children were given an extra week's holiday so that staff could clear space for classes. Fears that the Girls High School would be taken over proved false and notice was given that 'no society other than the Army and Navy has the authority to commandeer schools'. At Love Lane Infants, Marjory Betts would attend, often followed by her younger sister, the future Lady Barbara Castle, at a school built to accommodate 250 children but now, with the closure of the army-run barracks school, taking in up to 395 by 1916, spread into five classes of sixty and two smaller classes of forty-six and fifty-three taught in the school hall.

By 1917, scout camps had been set-up so that troops could work on farms during the summer.

Even at the start of the war, Miss Vickers was left to cope with an average of fifty-eight under-5s each day, but as war drew on, things became even worse. From the Upper School, teacher Fred Wheatley enlisted into the army and was away until invalided out having lost an arm in 1916. His colleague, Mr Pedelty, registered for the Home Hospital Reserve and was mobilised in the spring of 1915 so would be away until the spring of 1919. As a result, at times the headmaster, Mr Taylor, was teaching two classes simultaneously, shuttling back and forth between them throughout the day. It is hardly surprising that he was soon taken ill with exhaustion. Much teaching had to be done by 'pupil teachers', apprentices who worked in school for five years before attending teacher training. Classes included the usual subjects but most classrooms had maps to show the latest war news and children were often occupied sewing sandbags or mailbags for use at the front, knitting socks and scarves or, later in the war, out collecting chestnuts for processing into acetone to make explosives, or moss to be sterilised and used in wound dressings. A year after the war started, school hours were reduced to 9 to 11.45am and 1.15 to 3.25pm, because of fuel shortages for the ever-malfunctioning boiler (average classroom temperatures in the winter of 1915–16 were around freezing point). By 1917, attendances were falling. Periodic outbreaks of measles, mumps, whooping cough and chickenpox could mean the closure of the school for weeks at a time, but absences were growing even without these epidemics. Children were needed at home for a far more pressing problem – feeding the family.

As an island, Britain was heavily dependent on its imports, but the German U-Boat blockade sunk 169 merchant ships in April alone and averaged over 100 per month throughout the year, a total of 1,197 ships or 3,729,785 tons at a cost of 6,408 lives. In July, under pressure from the government and the Admiralty, General Haig launched the infamous Battle of Passchendaele as an attempt to break through the German lines in order to capture the U-Boat bases at Zeebrugge in the belief that, unless the submarine menace could be stopped, Britain might be starved into submission within a matter of months. According to government figures, in 1904 a family's food bill for a week cost 22s 6d. In July 1914, the cost was 25s but had risen by August to 29s and by December to 29s 3d. By December 1915, the same amount would cost 36s 6d and by May 1917 had rocketed to 50s 6d – a 100 per cent increase since July 1914. Put another way, the purchasing power of a sovereign spent on food dropped from 20s in August 1914 to just 9s 11d by May 1917. In an attempt to ensure supplies, the government set price limits on various essentials, setting the price of a loaf of bread at 9d but with wheat imports badly affected by the U-Boat blockade, that meant subsidising flour at a cost of £40,000,000 per year. Further subsidies were needed to ensure that farmers were able to sell potatoes at between £6 to £6.10s per ton to encourage production, as potatoes could be mixed with flour to make bread and help supplies stretch. Tea, butter and margarine supplies were disrupted everywhere and sugar was becoming increasingly scarce. Elsie MacIntyre, a munitions worker at Barnbow, recalled that for her: 'the most awful thing was food, it was very scarce. As we were coming off shift, someone would say, "There is a bit of steak at the butcher's." And I would get off the train and then go on the tram and I'd get off at Burley Road and run to the shop only to find a long queue and by the time it got to my turn there would be no more meat, only half a pound of sausage. You see, that's coming off night shifts, you went straight into a queue before you could go to bed. Then my mother would be in home needing half a stone of flour for the kids, you see. We were lucky if we got up to bed by 11a.m. and up again at four to catch the train, five o'clock to Barnbow.'

It became understood that if you saw a queue, you joined it simply because it meant a shop had supplies in. As queuing for food took up more and more time, mothers kept their children away from school to act as markers in the various lines outside local shops. Maud Cox was 8 years old in 1917: 'Mum took me up there and put me in the queue and she says, "Now stand still and don't move until I get the other ones away to school and I'll come back. But keep my place." Of course I was standing there and the snow was deep, it was right up over your feet. The next thing I knew, I was lying on a bench in the dairy. I'd fainted.'

Food queue, 1917. School attendances dropped as children were kept away to help mothers by joining the endless lines outside shops.

Coal rationing. The army was called in to help ensure that all families had access to fuel.

According to the Metropolitan Police, by early 1918 the average number of people standing in lines outside food shops on Saturdays was over 600,000 in London alone.

Allotments, once regarded as something of a fad, became highly sought-after as gardens, parks and even roadside verges were given over to food production. The Archbishop of Canterbury gave permission for Sunday working and some allotment sites even held church services while afternoon tea on the allotment became a common event. The number of thefts from allotments was such that guards were mounted and the penalty for stealing from someone else's plot was set at £100 or six months imprisonment. Soon, 3 million acres of extra land were under some form of cultivation, much of it worked by the newly formed Women's Land Army and by German prisoners-of-war.

A deputation of fish fryers headed to London from Bradford to demand help in easing the costs of buying potatoes on the basis that, between them, 303 shops were supplying up to 900,000 meals a week to workers at a cost of just 2d a time. Work canteens were set up to ensure that people could have at least one good meal per day as the government struggled to work out a fair system to safeguard food supplies. It took five months just to set up a system for rationing sugar, not helped by a lack of public awareness of what was going on: 'An amazing number of the [registration] forms, however,' reported *The Times*, 'were useless as returned, owing to the failure of householders to understand what they were required to do. Thousands of applicants instead of writing their own address on the line indicated for the purpose copied a fictitious address printed on posters and leaflets as a guide to the public. Further thousands gave no address at all, and every possible variety of error or omission that could be imagined was

Girl guides joined the effort to bring in the harvest every year as more and more farm labourers left for the forces.

The Women's Land Army was created in 1917 to cultivate millions of acres of extra land in parks and even roadsides that had been turned over to food production.

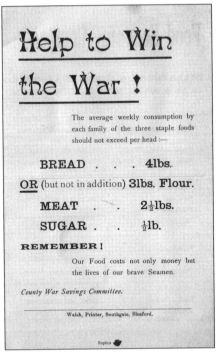

Help to Win the War !

The average weekly consumption by each family of the three staple foods should not exceed per head :—

BREAD . . . 4lbs.

OR (but not in addition) **3lbs. Flour.**

MEAT . . 2½lbs.

SUGAR . . ½lb.

REMEMBER !

Our Food costs not only money but the lives of our brave Seamen.

County War Savings Committee.

Walsh, Printer, Southgate, Sleaford.

Replica

Food Economy Campaign.

SYLLABUS of a Course of LESSONS to be given by MISS M. FERGUSSON

(With the consent of the Kesteven Education Committee).

Subject of Lesson.	Illustrative Dishes.
1. Bread and Flour Ration. Flour and Flour Substitutes.	Rice bread. Porridge. Barley scones. Maize pudding.
2. Explanation of Meat Ration. Stewing. Pot Roast. Meatless days.	Sea pie. Boned and stuffed breast of mutton. Dried green peas & cheese. Flaked maize and cheese.
3. Pulse Foods. Cereals. Flourless Puddings & Sauces.	Baked beans. Lentil and vegetable pie. Golden pudding & sauce. Ground rice or sago pudding
4. Stock. Soup. Vegetables. Potato Substitutes.	Lentil and tomato soup. Barley broth. Savoury rice. Oatmeal pudding.

Leaflets encouraging food economy. By 1917, government estimates feared Britain could soon be starved into submission as shipping losses peaked at around 100 cargo ships per month.

perpetrated.' As more and more items were added to the list of items to be rationed, confusion increased. Local schemes were put in place to manage a voluntary ration in which people were encouraged to cut back as far as possible, but when fats like butter and margarine grew increasingly hard to obtain, even in small quantities, official rationing was brought in, piloted in Sheffield where schoolchildren had been used to gather in a census of the resident population so that amounts for supplies could be worked out.

How much to allow was the subject of long debate. Clearly, it was argued, a miner would need more food than an office worker, but how much more? Eventually, it was proposed that men in heavy industry and agricultural work should get 8lb of bread per week, women doing similar work 5lb. Those men involved in 'ordinary' industry of manual work, 7lb, and those not working or doing 'sedentary' jobs, 4lb 8oz. Women in 'ordinary' industry should get 4lb and those in sedentary jobs 3lb 8oz. Children were to receive 'reasonable' rations but no one was clear what this actually meant. The shortage of wheat imported from overseas meant that bread came under the auspices of the Defence of the Realm Act, and wasting it became a criminal offence so that stale crusts could no longer be fed to chickens or ducks without risking a prison sentence. Rice could no longer be thrown at weddings without risking a stiff fine. Two 'meat free' days per week were introduced as a standard and free lectures were provided explaining how to use potatoes as flour for bread and puddings and offering cookery demonstrations for mothers at home. Vegetables were not rationed but some families found themselves using dandelion leaves instead of lettuce and foraging became a school activity. As well as finding chestnuts and moss: 'school children are everywhere employed gathering the blackberries in School hours under the control of their Teachers. The fruit is packed in baskets provided of regulation size, and sent by rail to the Army jam factories, while cheques are sent to the Teachers and payment authorized to the children of threepence per pound.' Nettles gathered from the same hedgerows could be boiled in salt water until nearly done, then two teaspoons of milk and a heaped teaspoon of butter or margarine added before bringing back to the boil. Alternatively they could be boiled, drained and placed in a pie dish with breadcrumbs, seasoning, a few spots of butter and a little cheese and then baked 'in a brisk oven for a few minutes'.

By then, the scale of rations had been set at 3oz bread and $\frac{1}{3}$oz butter for breakfast, 3oz meat 2oz bread and $\frac{1}{2}$oz butter for lunch with just $\frac{1}{7}$oz of sugar. Dinner was to be 3oz of meat, 3oz bread, 1oz flour, $\frac{1}{7}$oz sugar and $\frac{1}{3}$oz butter with an afternoon tea of $1\frac{1}{2}$oz of bread and $\frac{1}{4}$oz of sugar. The original scale of rations had allowed for $5\frac{1}{2}$lb of meat per person per week, but under Lord Rhondda's control, the Ministry for Food brought this down to just 1lb 14oz. 'The traditional character of the Englishman's breakfast,' reported *The Times History of the War* in 1918, 'was shattered by the disappearance of bacon from the meal, and the heavy meat tea favoured in the Northern counties became impossible.' Only restaurants serving meals for 1s 2d or less were exempt so that workers could get affordable meals.

Hoarding became a criminal offence and anyone deemed by their neighbours to have more than their fair share risked being reported to the police. A few cases did reach the courts based on gossip, but usually some form of evidence was needed before police raided the homes of suspected hoarders. Nevertheless, many housewives lived in fear that carefully managed stocks might be reported and it was even claimed that large-scale hoarders were destroying food rather than allowing it to be found so that a national amnesty was called to allow any excess stores to be surrendered to the local food committee as a way of avoiding the growing tensions between neighbours. Even with the amnesty, though, in 1918 there were 28,657 prosecutions for food offences in Great Britain, attracting fines averaging £4 7s 2d for offences ranging from allowing part of a loaf to go mouldy to couples inventing children to claim larger shares. In poorer areas, shops might every now and again find themselves 'rushed' by angry shoppers intent on looting whatever they could find.

Sir Arthur Yapp, a pillar of the Young Men's Christian Association, wrote to every school in the country to encourage headmasters to form a school legion of the Junior League of Safety with every member pledging:

I believe that I can help my country in all the following ways:
By eating enough – in order that I may grow up strong
By not eating more than enough and by eating very slowly.
By wasting nothing and damaging nothing; neither food nor any other material.
By being cheerful.
By signing this form and by wearing the anchor.

It didn't help that rumours circulated about Sir Arthur's hoarding of food but his grand notion met with little enthusiasm. Opponents of Lord Rhondda had a field day, with reports that he was hoarding tea, until it was shown that it was actually to supply a military hospital set up in his home. As Christmas approached, the traditional orange in the stocking now cost 6d each – four times the cost just four years earlier when a box of 200 would have cost just 10s 3d. Finding food was fast becoming a national obsession and food shortages a source of serious unrest. Strikes, already a frequent occurrence in industry, became common in protest at wages, living costs and food shortages.

In December 1916, Lloyd George became prime minister and brought in a new style of government. New ministries of food, food production, labour, National Service and shipping were set-up in requisitioned London clubs and began work in establishing, among others, a National Service Scheme to administer National Industrial Service with a view to replacing around 500,000 men taken from industry by the military with others who were unable to serve. By April, only 163,000 volunteers had registered and of those just 20,000 were placed in work. Like so much that was happening, it was widely seen as a futile exercise in bureaucracy. The scheme drew a great deal of criticism from trade unions angry about the 'dilution' of labour. Their skilled members, they argued, were being replaced by semi- or even unskilled workers with the threat of this leading to a lowering of wages that might continue after the war. Strikes broke out around the country as workers protested the ever-increasing restrictions of the Defence of the Realm Act (whisky could now only be bought between noon and 12.30 Monday to Friday), food shortages, high food prices, lack of housing for workers brought into towns by the National Industrial Service scheme, fatigue caused by long shifts and reduced holidays and delays in granting pensions and compensation to those wounded or injured in war service. Some strikes – like rent strikes aimed at protecting the families of servicemen overseas – enjoyed public sympathy, but others sometimes seemed petty and self-serving. When the Amalgamated Society of Engineers (ASE) went on strike in Sheffield to protect its members from call-up at the expense of non-union colleagues working in the same jobs, the Reverend George McNeal asked his congregation if the union had: 'remembered their privileges as well as their grievances. Grievances they had, but did they not think sufficiently of their privileges? Did they compare their position with the position of their brothers in the trenches – they themselves earning their four to six pounds a week (and that in perfect safety); their brothers on the battlefield targets for German guns day and night and earning a shilling a day?' Even some members of the

Society admitted to feeling embarrassed, especially when neighbours whose sons were fighting in France composed *A Prayer to Lloyd George* on behalf of the strikers:

> *Don't send me in the army George, I'm in the ASE.*
> *Take all the bloody labourers, but for God's sake don't take me.*
> *You want me for a soldier? Well that can never be*
> *A man of my ability – and in the ASE!*

Throughout 1916 and into 1917, those fit enough for the military were 'combed out' by periodic police and military sweeps through towns and at railway stations, cinemas and sporting events in search of young men without the proper exemption papers who could be taken into the forces. Matters came to a head in Castleford in August when 2,000 men walked out of Glasshoughton Pit in protest at the calling-up of some local miners. The strike soon spread to other pits and a meeting was held at the Prince of Wales Colliery to discuss the grievance. The miners, according to the *Yorkshire Evening Post*, had no objection to the calling-up of 'shirkers', but objected to the conscription of young men aged 18–23 who had worked in the pits since childhood when men who had come into mining since August 1914 were being left at home. Claiming that favouritism was keeping some at home who should be overseas, no notice was given of the strike and even the Yorkshire Miner's Association held back from supporting the action, saying that 'local actions had been taken without the men fully realising the situation'.

Very early in the war it was noted that production had slowed. In shipyards, a naval refit was now likely to take longer than in peacetime for the simple reason that men could earn enough in weekend overtime to not need to turn up for weekday shifts. A labour shortage meant overtime and potentially higher wages, which in turn meant workers could meet their needs with less work. It was a problem across all industries: 'There used to be a train go this way to Barnbow, a train go that way to York,' remembered Elsie Slater, 'and half of them that come from Castleford used to buzz on to York with the soldiers. There used to be no end of 'em forget to go to work and get on with the soldiers ... Oh they were fast, yeah, they never turned up.'

All this talk about being combed out— I get combed out every night, and I'm not allowed to say a word!

Periodic sweeps of public areas and even factories were carried out by the police and military to 'comb out' men of military age who might be trying to avoid answering their call-up.

In response, special 'munitions courts' were set up to hear cases brought by employers against their workforces. Despite restrictions on pub opening hours, a surprising number of munitions and engineering workers seem to have turned up for morning shifts – if they turned up at all – the worse for drink. Some became belligerent and threatened their supervisors and fellow workers or caused accidents, all of which could land them in court. In October 1915, five men from

Glasshoughton were summonsed to court for absenteeism and fined 32s each – the cost of the wages they would have earned. The court heard that in the first year of war alone Glasshoughton Pit had already lost almost 1,000 men to the army and that production was badly affected. Since April, it was reported, of the 1,062 men employed at the pit, 375 had worked no more than four shifts per week and the mine had lost 37,363 working days through absenteeism running at 23 per cent of the workforce as opposed to the 5 per cent agreed as a reasonable rate. April saw shortages of coal in London and by the end of the year, domestic coal was rationed. The comments of the Yorkshire Miners Association that the local men did not realise the situation was valid. Few people did realise the true situation in 1917. Those who did were extremely worried.

CHAPTER 5

'It would either kill you or just go...'

In July 1917, the Bishop of London told the *Daily Telegraph* that during 1915, nine soldiers had died every hour. A terrible statistic but, he said, during that period twelve babies in Britain had also died every hour and concluded 'it was more dangerous to be a baby than a soldier'. Poverty, food and fuel shortages all contributed to the situation. Since the comment was made, things had got even worse. Coal rationing had been introduced to help ensure fuel supplies but families were often left without heating. At the Love Lane schools, where the

Love Lane School, where a dwindling number of teachers struggled to keep classes running as temperatures fell to freezing.

temperamental boiler frequently broke down even when fuel was available, classes over that winter were held in temperatures barely warmer than sitting outdoors, and the thermometer in one classroom barely reached above −2 degrees Centigrade.

Prospects at the start of the new year seemed bleak and it seemed that British resolve was crumbling. Rationing had been introduced, guaranteeing supplies of basics like butter, tea and sugar, and it had eased the problem of spending so much time in food queues, but it could only work if there was food to be had and suppliers to get it from. On Monday, 7 January, all but one of the staff of the Castleford Co-operative Industrial Society were out on strike over pay and shops in Castleford, Normanton, Micklefield and Whitwood Mere were all closed. Their Pontefract colleagues at the Co-operative Wholesale Society had already been out for three weeks in a separate dispute. That

As shortages became worse, food economy drives encouraged already hungry people to eat even less.

weekend, and the following Saturday, none of Pontefract's butcher shops was open due to a shortage of meat. A few shops in Castleford were open but the quality of some of their products was a little dubious. William Cooke and William Stoker both found themselves in court for selling 'unsound meat' after Stoker killed an ailing cow and the two men sold on meat that the Sanitary Committee declared unfit for human consumption. In a statement hardly calculated to help his case, Cooke cheerfully told the committee he 'had sent lots of worse meat to Leeds', but still got away with a fine of 32 shillings. In an attempt to ease the food problem, communal kitchens were established. Two were set up in council schools in Castleford, two more in Whitwood schools and Glasshoughton and Ferry Fryston followed suit with one each to allow workers and their families to ensure at least one full meal a day at a reasonable price. As the shortages grew worse, people turned to whatever foods they could get hold of and February saw an outbreak of Enteric Fever in Castleford, later traced to supplies of mussels from the River Lune.

Before you light a fire THINK

Think of the men fighting in the sodden trenches. Think of the Italian soldiers in the snows. Think of the wounded in hospital. Think of someone fighting who is very dear to you. Remember that *the more coal for you the less coal for them*. Then see if you cannot do without that fire you meant to light. Follow the rule, one family one fire. The days you have a fire in the kitchen—sit in the kitchen. You can only burn your coal once. Every fire you save now you will be glad of later on.

Put off lighting the fire as long as you can—and put it out immediately you have done with it.

The coal you are going without is forging the key to VICTORY

Issued by the Coal Mines Dept., Board of Trade, Holborn Viaduct, E.C.1.

As fuel shortages grew worse, appeals were made to reduce the amount of coal used.

Out in France, the local Territorials had been thrown into a state of upheaval. Having pressured General Haig into launching the Passchendaele offensive, Prime Minister Lloyd George and his cabinet were now refusing to allow large numbers of reinforcements to be sent out to France to bring the army back up to strength after heavy losses during the battle. To make matters worse, in early October 1917, Lloyd George had ordered Haig to consider an extension of the line on the Western Front. What he did not mention at the time was that he had already agreed the extension with the French and was not asking Haig whether it was advisable or even possible. Lloyd George wanted it done. When Haig reported back on 8 October, it was in the knowledge that he was short of over 70,000 infantrymen with equivalent shortages in every branch of the army. He proposed that in view of the now-doubtful power of the French Army to resist a serious German attack, all other British fronts should be placed on the defensive and that all efforts should be made to bring the sixty-two British divisions in France up to strength so they could defend the line they already held. There simply were not enough troops to extend the line any further.

The next month, the War Office informed Haig that they wanted him to extend the line but would not be able to replace expected losses for the coming months and warned that the manpower crisis would only get worse. Conscription was bringing in thousands of extra men, but the War Cabinet had its own ideas about how to use them. They needed to balance military and industrial needs and had decided to prioritise defence of Britain over attacking the Germans. The cabinet was made up of politicians and did not contain anyone representing the military but announced that the priority for manpower should be firstly the fighting needs of the navy and air force. Secondly, providing a shipbuilding workforce to replace merchant navy losses. Thirdly, directing workers to tank and aeroplane production. And fourthly, to food production and timber felling. The army did not rate even a mention. Meanwhile, eight full divisions and another thirteen battalions of cyclists were to remain in England to defend against the remote possibility of a German invasion or of a Dublin-style uprising. Haig, meanwhile, was ordered to divert five of his already hard-pressed divisions to support the fighting in Italy.

On 24 November 1917, Haig advised the War Office that unless more troops were forthcoming he would have to break up fifteen of the fifty-seven divisions left in France just to bring the remaining formations back up to strength. The cabinet committee on manpower disagreed and proposed an alternative, ordering a reduction from twelve infantry battalions in every division to nine. The military members of the army council protested against the suggestion on the basis that it affected every regiment of the infantry and cut straight through the organisational structure for which every officer and man had been trained and on which all supply and planning calculations were based. All that proposal actually meant was that the British would still have the same number of divisions on paper, but far fewer troops in each one. Even though the number of troops available to him were dwindling, Haig knew the German army was expanding after the Russian revolution had ended fighting on the Eastern Front, freeing many thousands of Germans to reinforce the Western Front.

As a result of the decision, entire battalions were erased at a stroke and the regimental spirit that had held them together destroyed as brigades and divisions were disbanded. For the 1/5th, the re-organisation meant leaving 49th Division for amalgamation with the 2/5th to become simply 5th KOYLI as part of 62nd Division. By now the links with Pontefract and Castleford had been eroded, but there were still plenty of local men in the ranks to retain its links with the area, although plenty now came from further afield with Sheffield and Leeds providing many of the replacements sent out from England.

Early 1918 saw the roads of France filled with dislocated units as battalions moved from one division to another. That was when the Germans launched their last-ditch effort to break the British lines before American troops arrived in France in sufficient numbers to turn the tide. In just five hours on 21 March, 1,100,000 shells rained down on the weak spot between the British and French armies. Close behind the barrage came 'stormtroopers' drawn from the best and most experienced German infantrymen available, armed with flamethrowers and machine-guns. Their job was not to attack strongpoints but to infiltrate into rear areas to attack headquarters, artillery positions and supply depots, spreading panic behind the British lines. On the first day alone, the 'Kaiserschlacht' (Emperor's Battle) killed around 20,000 British troops and wounded about 35,000, a figure only slightly less than the first day of the Somme. Soon, the British Fifth Army was in full retreat.

On the day that the Germans launched their offensive, Lloyd George reported to Parliament that the British Army had been stronger in January 1918 than it had been a year earlier. Technically, he was right but almost 300,000 of the extra men were non-combatant labour troops and 80,000 more were in non-fighting roles. The number of

Wounded British soldiers captured during the 1918 spring offensive await transport to prison camps in Germany.

By 1918, the need for more troops meant that the minimum age for service overseas was dropped to 18½ years.

infantrymen available to actually fight the enemy had dropped by 100,000. A few days later, a government statement about reports that extending the line had caused the disaster claimed: 'There is not the smallest justification for the suggestion that this portion of the line was taken over contrary to the judgement of Sir William Robertson and Sir Douglas Haig.' While Major-General Frederick Maurice, director of military operations, openly disputed this in the press and asked for a public enquiry, Haig privately noted: 'no one can be both a soldier and a politician at the same time. We soldiers have to do our duty and keep silent, trusting Ministers to protect us.' It was a loyalty not shared by the ministers. Maurice was sacked a few days later and denied the court-martial he had requested to give him chance to present the facts of the matter. No enquiry ever took place. Meanwhile, Haig and his staff were left trying desperately to avoid a major defeat.

For the KOYLIs of 62nd Division, the attack began near the village of Bucquoy early on 27 March, when large numbers of German troops could be seen massing in a sunken road between Hebuterne and Rossignol Wood. The attack, when it came, forced 2/4th KOYLI back from their trenches and the 5th were quickly brought up to reinforce them. At dawn the next morning, a counter-attack began. The War Diary of the 2/4th records what happened next:

'D' [Company] and the 5th Bn [Companies] gained their objectives. They were then cut off and nothing was heard of them after 8am.

The 5th battalion diary noted the initial success but adds: 'A', 'B' and 'C' companies cut off by the enemy and are missing.' Behind those simple words lies the fact that the four companies sent forward had between them lost twenty-two officers and 716 men in a matter of hours, among them Lieutenant Colonel OCS Watson, killed as he attempted to cover his men's withdrawal from trenches overrun by the Germans, and Harold Brookes, only son of Arthur and Sarah Ann of Old Church, Pontefract. So, too, were other Pontefract men: Albert Butterfield, only son of widowed Harriet of Elm Street in Grovetown, Peter Fieldhouse, James France, William Foster of Cutsyke and

Bucquoy Cemetery near Arras. It was near here that 5ᵗʰ KOYLI fought the massed attacks of the German Spring Offensive, 1918.

Sergeant James Walker, winner of the Military Medal for gallantry were all listed as killed.

The situation was desperate. A special 'Order of the Day' was issued by General Headquarters:

To:

ALL RANKS OF THE BRITISH ARMY IN FRANCE AND FLANDERS

Three weeks ago to-day the enemy began his terrific attacks against us on a fifty-mile front. His objects are to separate us from the French, to take the Channel Ports and destroy the British Army.

In spite of throwing already 106 Divisions into the battle and enduring the most reckless sacrifice of human life, he has as yet made little progress towards his goals.

We owe this to the determined fighting and self-sacrifice of our troops. Words fail me to express the admiration which I feel for the splendid resistance offered by all ranks of our Army under the most trying circumstances.

Many amongst us now are tired. To those I would say that Victory will belong to the side which holds out the longest. The French Army is moving rapidly and in great force to our support.

There is no other course open to us but to fight it out. Every position must be held to the last man: there must be no retirement. With our backs to the wall and believing in the justice of our cause each one of us must fight on to the end. The safety of our homes and the Freedom of mankind alike depend upon the conduct of each one of us at this critical moment.

(Signed) D. Haig F. M. Commander-in-Chief British Armies in France

General Headquarters Tuesday, April 11th, 1918

That evening, the miners of 12th Battalion Kings Own Yorkshire Light Infantry were ordered to cover the crossroads at La Couronne to Bleu and endeavour to gain touch with the 95th Brigade on their left flank under the command of the Guards Brigade. Holding the line was considered to be critical and the men ordered to hold on at all costs.

A typical week's losses, 1918

Four times the 12th held back massed German attacks, but gradually they were forced back. Earning the nickname 'the Yorkshire Guards', the 12th eventually had to retreat but only after losing over half their men killed, wounded or captured, among them Castleford men 40-year-old Sam Asprey of Duke Street, and 38-year-old Leonard Wood, from West Street, both killed together on the 13th.

The crisis raised fears of an invasion and thousands of Volunteer Training Corps men were mobilised to strengthen the east coast defences. Munitions workers gave up their breaks to keep the troops supplied and agreed to forego holiday time. Meanwhile, a new Manpower Bill was rushed through Parliament to remove the youngest age groups of men eligible for conscription from previously protected jobs. The upper age was raised to 50, but specialists like doctors could be even older. In May, all men born between 1898 and 1899 were called-up, regardless of their occupation, and a month later, the scheme was expanded to those born between 1895 and 1897, the only exceptions being shipyard workers and those in the oil shale industry. Over 100,000 munitions workers and 50,000 miners were released for the army but the move inevitably caused resentment.

In May, 5,000 men walked out of Wheldale Pit in protest at the suggestion that men aged under 32 who were the only sons of dependent parents or whose family had already sent half their sons to war should be made exempt from the ballot held to determine who would be called-up under the new rules. The Yorkshire Miners Association advised them that the exemptions had been agreed by the union and that the strike was unofficial, advising them to return to work. They did, but only for a few weeks before Wheldale miners walked out again, this time in a dispute over allowances paid to the families of former miners serving in the forces. Early in the war, local employers had agreed to pay 5 shillings per week and provide free house coal to help support the families of those miners who chose to enlist, but had set an end date of September 1915 as the cut-off point for volunteering. The offer was not open to those called-up under the Derby Scheme or the Military Service Act. The National Registration census of October 1915 was the precursor to full conscription and management felt that goodwill payments to volunteers was one thing, but making payments to support men who had come into mining as an alternative to military service who then found themselves conscripted was not something they could support. As it was, they argued, the payments amounted to £7,500 per year and with lower production, no export trade and high levels of absenteeism, this was difficult enough to maintain. The strikers had set-up a union subscription to donate a shilling per week per child of former colleagues and this alone was costing another £2,850 per year. The action quickly spread to Glasshoughton, Fryston and Pontefract, and by the end of June, 12,000 workers were out in the Pontefract district. At a meeting on 1 July in the Queen's Theatre in Castleford, the strikers heard that management had agreed to provide coal to dependents of all former pit men currently serving. It would be almost six weeks before the next strike, over the issue of whether meal breaks were included in the agreed fifty-four hour working week. All but eighteen pits in Yorkshire were closed and around 80,000 men out. It was not just a local problem. Strikes broke out across the country in pits, munitions factories and even 14,000 officers of the Metropolitan Police refused to work, which led to the deployment of soldiers of the Guards and the Special Constabulary being brought in to maintain order in the capital. Another police strike was threatened in Manchester and in Birmingham 100,000 engineers walked out in their own dispute.

Meanwhile, out in France, survivors of the 5th KOYLI were again on the move, this time into the Champagne region north-east of Paris. In 1914, German troops reached the Marne river and had only been held back by the 'miracle of the Marne'. French troops were loaded into Parisian taxis and rushed to prevent a breakthrough that would have seen the Germans marching into Paris itself. Now, the massive spring offensive had again seen them push forward to the Marne. Huge artillery pieces were so close they could send shells into the city centre and a multi-national force of French, British, American and Italian troops were massing for a counter-attack. The British 62nd Division was one of those sent to help.

On 20 July, 5th KOYLI, along with their 2/4th colleagues and men of the West Yorkshires and the Duke of Wellington's Regiment pressed forward into the Bois de Reims, a forest so thick that one senior

Heavily camouflaged German troops in position. The men of 62nd Division would suffer heavily as they sought to clear the thick woods along the Marne in 1918.

commander compared it to the Burmese jungle, where he had served a few years earlier. Far from the desolation of the trench lines, the Second Battle of the Marne would be fought in the open, through fields filled with standing corn and through dense woods. As the official history explained, 'it was very evident that the barrage had affected the enemy not at all, for everywhere his machine guns poured a perpetual hail of bullets into the waves of advancing Yorkshiremen'. For the men, the worst of it was that the guns could not be located. They were very skilfully hidden among the trees and corn, firing low to scythe through the legs of the attackers, forcing them to drop into the path of the bullets. 'It was an invisible foe which we were pitted against,' an officer of the battalion later explained, 'and very few of us ever caught sight of a Boche.' In the woods, Lieutenant Burrows of the West Yorkshires recalled that:

[C]*areful direction and keeping of formations soon became impossible. The thick undergrowth, some quite impassable, prevented any intelligent observation. Our own scouts sometimes carefully stalked each other. Then the Boches decided to join in at the game. A machine gun would spit out from some cunningly concealed position. At times an ingenious sniper would fire at us from his fortalice in some tree-top ... Though it was quite light, the further we wormed our way into this tangle of wood the more 'nervy' we became ... Once we had gone forward only to find a whole crowd of Boche behind us. We changed direction to avoid being cut off. This game of hide and seek continued for hours. The wood was certainly held in strength. The nervous excitement of scrambling through undergrowth, sometimes meeting a terrified Hun popping up from some hole, or sometimes finding oneself in the centre of an amazed group of attacking Germans, was rather wearing. Naturally enough the men were feeling exhausted. We had done our main task, for the edge of the wood had been cleared of enemy machine guns ... However, we made another attempt, but only ran into many more Boches. Our next excitement was to run into some French, but fortunately no side suffered casualties. Then we tried a joint effort, but with no better success. The game was no nearer solution. We decided to hold on to the southern edge of the wood, for it was hopeless attempting too much.*

The thick woods hid the bodies of those killed just as surely as the mud of Flanders. James Makin from Featherstone was 19 when he died and has no known grave. Nor does 20-year-old George Jackson of Tanshelf. In Castleford, the family of 19-year-old Arthur Gaffney received news of his death around the same time as the families of William Turner and Thomas Wilson. Pontefract lost Harry Athorn, Charles Cross, J. Tipling, Richard Goodall, Frank Parr and Fred Newitt, among others. The battle, though hardly likely to have been seen as such by the bereaved, was a success. The Germans were pushed back and it marked the beginning of the end. The Battle of Amiens on 8 August went down in history as the black day of the German Army, and from then on, the

British pushed forward relentlessly. All the lessons of the past four years had been learned. Casualties were heavy but slowly, the war was coming to an end.

In August, Castleford's VC winner was again in the papers, this time for heroism away from the battlefield. He was convalescing from wounds and illness at a hospital in Norwich when 3-year-old Phyllis Richardson fell into the river at Thorpe and would have drowned had Thomas Bryan not seen what happened and rescued her, providing first aid until she could be taken to hospital. Bryan's heroism, though, was seen in marked contrast to the behaviour of the area's younger men. Petty crime had soared and Pontefract's cricket pavilion had been vandalised, much to the disgust of magistrate F.W. Tempest, who asked what those former cricketers now serving overseas would think if they knew. Police Superintendent Akroyd knew exactly where the blame lay. With their fathers away, it was the court's responsibility to instil discipline and greater use of the birch would no doubt help. A prime culprit in the moral collapse of Pontefract and Castleford was quickly identified – too much cinema. Too many youngsters, he said, were influenced by what they saw on the screen. Soon, though, even the heinous attack on local cricket would be forgotten as Pontefract became the centre of a national story.

On the afternoon of Friday, 16 August, Wesleyan Minister George Neal Willis was visiting a Miss Sykes when they heard a frantic knocking on the door. Answering it, they found a distraught Gertrude Lawn, who asked them to come with her. She had been on her way home from a trip to the bank when she noticed that the window display of her landlady's shop had been disturbed. Gertrude knew that her landlady, 62-year-old Rhoda Walker, had been preparing to go away on holiday and she had been tidying her jeweller's shop when Gertrude had stopped by earlier, so it was unusual for the display to be in a mess. Finding the front door locked, Gertrude went around to the back and let herself in. There, in a pool of blood and surrounded by her shattered dentures, lay Rhoda. Drawers and trays of jewellery were strewn around the floor. Hurrying back with Gertrude to the shop, Willis saw what had happened and immediately sent for a local nurse who, in turn, called for an ambulance. Rhoda was bleeding heavily and barely

Under renovation, Rhoda Walker's shop is now a restaurant.

breathing. She died twelve hours later, murmuring 'oh George' three times before passing away. It was evident from her injuries that her death was not accidental. A murder enquiry began.

Detective Sergeant Fred Wright was sent to investigate the crime and a search of the property revealed a lady's blouse and underskirt stained with blood alongside a bowl of blood-stained water where someone had tried to clean their hands. The shop, standing on the busy Town End junction, was well-known. Witnesses came forward and, piece by piece, Sergeant Wright began to put together the story of what had happened.

Thomas Driver of Carleton had passed the shop at about 3pm and had seen a hand, presumably Rhoda's, arranging a display in the window. At about 3.55pm, Kathleen Benstead and her sister, Rebecca Large, had passed the shop and noticed a soldier standing outside. Kathleen's husband was a gunner and she noticed the six wound stripes on the man's sleeve. As they continued up the hill into town, they passed the post lady, Alice Poppleton, on her rounds coming the other way. Alice went into the shop but saw no one. She called out 'Post, Mrs Walker', and left it on the counter. Mention of the soldier reminded PC Huck that he had seen two soldiers near Barnsley Road at about 3.25pm and had recognised them as George Cardwell and Percy Barrett, both of whom had been in the area for around three months and had been working at Hemsworth Colliery. Barrett had been carrying a thick wooden walking stick when Huck saw him.

Sergeant Wright and PC Huck went to Scot's Cottages in Ackworth Moor Top on Monday to speak to Ann Pratt. Ms Pratt told them that George Cardwell was her brother and had turned up unexpectedly on her doorstep fifteen years after she had last seen him as a child. He told her that he and Barrett were on extended leave and asked her to put them up for a while. The two men took jobs at Hemsworth Colliery, sometimes working in civilian clothes with their wound stripes on the sleeves, at other times walking around in uniform. On the day in question they had got up around lunchtime and told her they were going into Pontefract. They had returned around teatime, had a meal and left, telling her they would be gone for two days. Since then she had not seen them but a money order for 29 shillings had arrived that morning.

With the case now making national headlines, Cardwell's mother contacted Halifax police. The two men had visited her on Saturday, when Barrett had asked her to pawn a gold ring for him, saying it had belonged to his now dead brother. Later, Mrs Cardwell found two more gold rings and immediately suspected what had happened. She gave police an address in London she thought they would head for.

On 20 August, Detective Sergeant George Whitmore arrested Cardwell on Murdyke Street, just off the Old Kent Road, and found blood-encrusted jewellery in his pocket. Soon after, Detective Sergeant Bertie Sims recognised Barrett and found eighteen brooches, twenty-five gold rings, eighteen silver rings, five gold lockets and seven gold pendants in his possession. Barrett immediately began to blame Cardwell. The next day, accompanied by DS Wright, the two men arrived at Baghill Station and were transported through a crowd of onlookers, who booed and hissed at them as they passed. In a court filled to capacity, the two were remanded in custody at Armley Prison awaiting their trial. Both set out to blame the other. In September, Barrett wrote a statement in which he said he remained outside while Cardwell went into the shop. He amended this to say he had gone into the shop and used Cardwell's name – perhaps explaining Rhoda's dying words. The trial was set for 18 December and the case adjourned.

That autumn, as Cardwell and Barrett settled into cells at Armley, the news from France was good. Advances were being made and everywhere the Germans were being pushed back all along the Western Front. At home, though, reports were coming in of an increasing number of cases of a new strain of influenza. There had been sporadic outbreaks throughout the war, including one in March, but this was different. In the United States, army doctor Roy Grist was working at Camp Devens near Boston:

These men start with what appears to be an ordinary attack of la grippe or influenza, and when brought to the hospital they very rapidly develop the most vicious type of pneumonia that has ever been seen. Two hours after admission they have the mahogany spots over the cheekbones, and a few hours later you can begin to see cyanosis extending from their ears and spreading all over the face, until it is hard to distinguish the colored men from the white ... It is only a matter of a few hours then until death comes ... It is horrible. One can stand it to see one, two, or twenty men die, but to see these poor devils dropping like flies ... We have been averaging a hundred deaths per day ... It takes special trains to carry away the dead. For several days there were no coffins.

Widely known as Spanish Flu because neutral Spain had no press censorship and could report freely on the worldwide epidemic, the symptoms shown by its victims soon gained it a new nickname – 'the blue death'. It struck with such devastating speed that someone symptom-free at breakfast could be dead by evening and, unlike other strains, this flu appeared to strike healthy young people aged 20–30 more than the young or old and, it seemed, those who should have had the strongest immune systems were, unexpectedly, the most vulnerable.

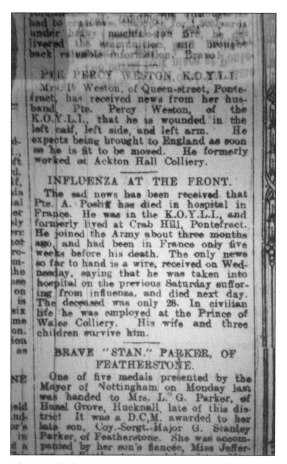

had to craw over sand in for 1,500 yards under heavy machine-gun fire, he delivered the ammunition, and brought back valuable information. Bravo l...

PTE. PERCY WESTON, K.O.Y.L.I.

Mrs. P. Weston, of Queen-street, Pontefract, has received news from her husband Pte. Percy Weston, of the K.O.Y.L.I., that he is wounded in the left calf, left side, and left arm. He expects being brought to England as soon as he is fit to be moved. He formerly worked at Ackton Hall Colliery.

INFLUENZA AT THE FRONT.

The sad news has been received that Pte. A. Poshiff has died in hospital in France. He was in the K.O.Y.L.I., and formerly lived at Crab Hill, Pontefract. He joined the Army about three months ago, and had been in France only five weeks before his death. The only news so far to hand is a wire, received on Wednesday, saying that he was taken into hospital on the previous Saturday suffering from influenza, and died next day. The deceased was only 28. In civilian life he was employed at the Prince of Wales Colliery. His wife and three children survive him.

BRAVE "STAN." PARKER, OF FEATHERSTONE.

One of five medals presented by the Mayor of Nottingham on Monday last was handed to Mrs. L. G. Parker, of Hazel Grove, Hucknall, late of this district. It was a D.C.M. awarded to her late son, Coy.-Sergt.-Major G. Stanley Parker, of Featherstone. She was accompanied by her son's fiancée, Miss Jeffer-

Influenza struck not only those left behind but killed thousands of soldiers too.

Troops in the front lines came to regard being hospitalised as a virtual death sentence. As one survivor later recalled:

It didn't last long – it would either kill you, or just go. The ones that went into hospital, we were hearing the day afterwards that they'd died. It would kill you in twenty-four hours – two days at most. That's when men started refusing to go into hospital. I know we lost more men from flu, day for day, than we did during the war.

At home, special measures were put in place. In October, the headmaster of Love Lane school had just one member of staff and 100 children able to attend and in many areas schools closed completely for weeks at a time. Cinemas, churches and shops emptied as people sought to avoid contact with potential carriers, and the papers were filled with adverts like those for Veno's Lightning Cough Cure, promising 'instantaneous relief', or preventatives like Jeyes Fluid, which was recommended for spraying 'the atmosphere of the office, factory, home and cinema ... disinfect lavatories, sinks and drains'. The *News of the World* advised readers to 'wash inside the nose with soap and water each night and morning: force yourself to sneeze night and morning, then breathe deeply; do not wear a muffler; take sharp walks regularly and walk home from work; do not "dope"; eat plenty of porridge'. None of which helped. The *Yorkshire Evening Post* was more practical: 'Do not ignore a feverish cold, no matter how slight the symptoms may be ... Go to bed and remain there until the symptoms abate. Keep entirely apart from children and old people ... use your common sense under all circumstances, and think of others.'

In the wake of a minor outbreak earlier in the year, Dr Hartley, medical superintendent of the Normanton and District Joint Isolation Hospital, told the committee that quinine and cinnamon had both been put forward as a cure but, in his opinion, a ban on the: 'pernicious habit of kissing would be more efficacious. Probably the unnecessary amount of kissing prevalent today might be attributed to a flood of sentiment let loose by the war. In urgent cases, where total abolition would be a hardship, a small book of kissing coupons could be allowed provided that proper antiseptic precautions were taken.' The tongue in cheek suggestion seemed less outlandish in the current crisis when councils applied for military exemptions for their gravediggers and called in soldiers to help keep pace with burying the dead. The Sanitary Committee agreed the closure of all schools and Sunday Schools and the banning of children from places of entertainment for at least two weeks in an attempt to contain the spread of the disease.

Figures for the Pontefract and Castleford district were not published but every week the paper contained stories of local people who had fallen victim. In Ackworth, where influenza was 'still rife' and where there had been 'many deaths', Frank Seal was already in mourning for his wife when he buried his daughter. Mrs Harrison left a husband and eight children. Some measure of the scale of the disaster comes from Sheffield where the week up to 4 November had seen 468 people die – more in a single week than the Sheffield Pals battalion lost in the entire war. In neighbouring Leeds, 409 people died that week, 202 directly of influenza with 207 flu-related cases of complications like pneumonia. The death rate, it was reported, stood at 51.2 per thousand instead of the normal fifteen or sixteen. In all, between October 1918 and the end of the outbreak the following May, over 200,000 people were reported to have died, an average monthly death toll double that of the Western Front.

With the country still ravaged by the epidemic, the second week of November brought the longed-for news. On Monday, 11 November, crowds again began to gather in Carlton Street and Bank Street. This time it was not a mob intent on targeting shopkeepers but people who had heard rumours that something momentous was about to happen. The centre of attention was the post office, but the news, when it came shortly after 11.00am, came from the offices of the *Pontefract and Castleford Express* on Commercial Street. The paper later reported:

> *Those who read the great tidings that the armistice was signed at 5am and hostilities ceased at 11am appeared to be hardly able to credit it and all it meant at first scarcely realised. The news spread like wildfire around the town and decorations began to appear. While immense relief was evident that the tremendous strain and anxiety of the past four and a quarter years was now happily at an end, there were many who in this hour of victory and thanksgiving did not forget that for others the end of the war would bring back vivid memories of the sacrifice of their husbands, fathers and sons. Castleford has played its part in the Great War nobly and patriotically and its sons have served on all fronts.*

In Featherstone, flags were everywhere and in the evening bonfires were lit and 'miniature cannon and fireworks were discharged'.

Carlton Street and Bank Street, Castleford. It was here that crowds began to gather on the morning of 11 November 1918 to hear the news of the Armistice.

The same area today.

Munitions girls 'sang lustily, not at all perturbed that their occupation was practically gone'. A favourite song of the time, *When the boys come marching home*, was sung over and over, but 'what of the homes where the "boys" will return no more?' asked the *Express*:

> *The sense of loss was tempered by the knowledge that these lives had not been sacrificed in vain. And heard above the note of personal loss was surely gratitude that the sacrifice of human life was ended.*

In Knottingley a 'comic costume band' provided an impromptu concert and children spent the day building a huge bonfire and an effigy of the kaiser to sit atop it. Their parents attended a service of thanksgiving and took up a collection for local prisoners-of-war. Community kitchens served up a special 'Armistice Pudding', although unfortunately the recipe has since been lost.

Across in Pontefract, there was 'general rejoicing, though restrained, particularly early in the day'. Once the news was confirmed, though, 'greetings in the street were of the liveliest while smiles radiated from many a countenance which had rarely been so brightened during the past four years'. Church bells in every parish rang out for hours. As the day wore on, celebrations became noisier. Fireworks, banned since 1914, were let off to add to the noise of 'the firing of pistols and the like and the singing of groups of young people who doubtless felt it their duty to congregate in the streets, to traipse about in bands and indulge in songs that were supposed to express loyalty and gladness at the wonderful turn events had taken'. There was no organisation, just spontaneous outpourings of relief it was finally over. There was, noted the *Express*, 'no disorder worthy of notice'. It wasn't entirely true. The following week's paper described how 'certain residents of Moorthorpe entirely mistook the spirit of the day ... when, instead of observing the great armistice they fought like cats' in a dispute between neighbours.

For some, news of the armistice came too late. Richard Leng, 22-year-old winner of both the Distinguished Conduct Medal and Military Medal, and whose little brother Donald had been killed on the Somme after he lied about his age to enlist, was himself killed just three days before the armistice. On the same day, 21-year-old George Wilson died as a prisoner-of-war in Germany. As if to emphasise that this was a world war, 10 November had seen the deaths of Francis Wood in Kalamaria, Greece, and 20-year-old Harold Bailey in Italy. Even as news of the ceasefire came through, 27-year-old company quartermaster sergeant Ernest Firth passed away at a hospital in Etaples, and 28-year-old Tom Barker, invalided back for Home Service with the Labour Corps, died of flu. The war may have stopped, but the dying had not. As men began to clear the battlefields, accidents with unexploded ammunition took their toll, men succumbed to wounds sustained days or weeks earlier, and others fell victim to the flu epidemic now raging among the troops. On 17 November, John Stephens of 12 KOYLI and 21-year-old Thomas Walker of the Royal Garrison Artillery were among the dead. A week after the war ended, Henry Bradshaw died near Salonika. And so it went on. It was not until 31 December 1920 that the government finally stopped counting those who died 'in or as a result of the war'.

In December 1918, local men in the 5th KOYLI crossed into Germany itself.

On the night of the armistice, fires were lit and householders forgot the blackout. The lights were coming on again and families could look forward to Christmas. There would still be shortages, but even they could not diminish the relief. But despite the joyous singing, it would still be some time before the boys came marching home. A week after the armistice was signed, 5th KOYLI began its long march into Germany itself, crossing the border on 17 December. On Boxing Day 1918, the first contingent of KOYLI men left the small German town of Embken, finally heading for home.

CHAPTER 6

'... in perfect silence'

By early 1919, men in the forces and their families at home were becoming restless. They had signed on for the 'duration of war' and now it was over, they wanted to get on with their lives. Protests and 'soldier strikes' broke out in camps across England and France at the delay in releasing men back to civilian life. The Russian Revolution had created an atmosphere of fear across Europe and the British

The bonfire prepared for the peace celebrations, 1919.

Inauguration of Pontefract's war memorial, 1923.

Mayor and council staff outside Pontefract Town Hall, 1919.

Government were no exception. British troops were already deployed in Russia as part of an international force sent to help fight the Bolsheviks in an attempt to prevent the spread of communism to other countries, but fears were growing of some sort of revolution in Britain. The Volunteer Training Corps, formed as an amateur Home Guard, had developed into a well-trained and reliable force. The threat of invasion was gone but the force was not stood down, kept on hand in case of serious disturbances at home by Socialists inspired by the Russian example. Strikes across the country involved workers and even the police and a protest march of thousands of soldiers was stopped outside London by other soldiers armed with rifles and bayonets.

The problem was twofold: firstly the war was not over. The armistice was only a ceasefire and in Germany, the 5th KOYLI were warned that: 'if peace negotiations fail, notice of the termination of the Armistice in 72 hours will be given to the Germans. The day on which the Armistice ceases will be called "J" Day.' In other words, the war could resume at any time. At the same time, over 8 million men had served in the forces in the previous four years and getting them back into civilian life could not be accomplished overnight. Many had left their jobs to enlist and would be unemployed when they got home. Priority had to go to those who could administer the system, those who had jobs to go back to and those who would be of more value at home. Those who enlisted in 1914 thought they should be given priority, regardless of their circumstances, those conscripted in 1918 argued they had been called-up only for the period of hostilities.

Attempting to calm the situation, the German-born secretary of state for war, Lord Milner, explained that people should:

Remember that, though the fighting may have ceased, all is not yet over. Impatience and overhaste might yet rob us of all that four long years of unexampled struggle and sacrifice have won. We have yet to make a just, strong and enduring peace. When the representatives of Great Britain go to the Council table to negotiate that peace, they must not have a disarmed and disunited nation behind them. If we are all at sixes and sevens at home, if what remains of our Army is not compact, disciplined, orderly, we shall never get the sort of peace, which we justly

Peace celebrations in Carlton Street, Castleford.

expect. The world, which is still in many parts seething with disorder, may not settle down for years, or let us get back to normal life and work in safety and tranquillity ... Our guiding principle was to demobilise in the way most likely to lead to the steady resumption of industry, and to minimise the danger of unemployment. Pivotal men first, basic industries like coal mining before those of less vital importance. In each industry those men first, who were assured of immediate employment. Subject to these ruling principles, we want to release the older men, and those of longest service, before the younger ones. That is the general idea. I don't say that it can ever be perfectly executed. Certainly the execution isn't perfect yet. When the huge engine began to move, some defects immediately appeared in the machinery. These are being remedied. Some officials may have been stupid or obstructive. I am afraid, where thousands of people have to co-operate, there will always be a good sprinkling of muddlers. But when all is said and done the big engine is moving. It is moving at a steadily increasing pace.'

As people waited for news of when the war would finally be over, the murder of Rhoda Walker was again making national headlines. The trial of Cardwell and Barrett had begun on 3 December, with each man still blaming the other. At the Assizes, Barrett had complained about newspaper coverage claiming he was 23 years old when, he said, he was only 19. His barrister then gave his age at trial as 21, making it difficult for the jury to rely on much of what Barrett told them. He admitted to having been outside the shop but said it was Cardwell who went in. Cardwell said he had sent Barrett into the shop to buy a watch key and knew nothing about the attack until he saw a bloodstained hand grabbing rings from the window. Witness Kathleen Benstead had noticed a man with six wound stripes standing outside. Cardwell had six, Barrett had two. Barrett's sister had reported that he had the large walking stick seen by PC Huck that was suspected of having caused the injuries. The jury had to choose. Both men had been in the shop but each said the other had committed the crime. Rhoda's last words, 'oh George', suggested that Cardwell had played some part in it, and

Unveiling of Knottingley's War Memorial, 1921.

he had even admitted to having held a cushion over her face to gag her after she had been beaten by Barrett. They could find one guilty of the murder and the other of being an accomplice, but which story should they believe? In the end they decided both were equally guilty of a vicious attack on an elderly widow. Their appeal failed and on 8 January 1919, executioner Albert Pierrepoint travelled to Armley Gaol to carry out sentence on Cardwell and Barrett, forever after known in Pontefract as 'the hung two'.

Slowly, things began to return to some sort of normality. The Castleford Food Control Committee remained in operation, Councillor Pringle complaining that bacon supplies were 'a real winking business', but while he had found bacon that 'was not very nice, no conscientious man could say it was unfit for food'. Returning soldiers had created even more demand on the stocks available for a time, but increasing supplies meant that it was hoped all rationing would end soon. Tea was removed from the ration in December.

Men came home and went back to work, but that too caused disruption. Around 5,000 women in the Castleford area alone had worked in munitions and were now about to be laid-off. Former munitionette Helen Bagnall of Castleford wrote to complain that one of her colleagues had told her 'I am ashamed to let it be known that I have worked at Barnbow because wherever we go in the town we are jeered at, sneered at and insulted by men because they say we have no right to the Government's promise of 3s 9d a day for a few weeks or until we can find employment'. Surely, she argued, the men of Castleford would not begrudge them thirteen weeks of pay until they could find work elsewhere.

Then on 28 June, exactly five years after that fateful shot in Sarajevo, a peace treaty was signed at Versailles. The war was over. Unlike the armistice, the peace celebrations were organised and lavish. On Saturday, 19 July, Knottingley began its celebrations: 'Not since the Coronation of King George,' wrote the *Express*, 'has the spirit of enjoyment been so manifest throughout the town. The procession in the afternoon, the tea, and the sports, all lent themselves to making a happy time for all who cared to take part. Many householders and shopkeepers had been at great pains to decorate their premises, and there was bunting of some sort displayed from most of the buildings. The inhabitants made the most of a day's jubilation, and light dresses

SHAW—In ever loving memory of a dear husband and dad, Sergt. George Shaw, K.O.Y.L.I., killed in action on the Cambrai Front, Nov. 20th, 1917, aged 28 years.

His children are always recalling his name,
As they look at his photo that hangs in a frame;
And then, with their eyes full of tears, they will say,
"Oh, why did they take our dear daddy away."
Gone and forgotten by some he may be,
But never on earth by his children and me.
From memory's page we'll never blot
Three little words, "Forget him not."
—From his loving Wife and Children, Sissy, Donald. Wilfred, 2, Argyle-street, Normanton Common.

STONES—In loving memory of our dear son and brother, Gunner Bernard Stones, of York-street, Tanshelf, who died Nov. 16th, 1917, of wounds received

To do his bit and take his share;
His heart was good, his spirit brave,
His resting-place a hero's grave.
—From his sorrowing Sister and Brother-in-law, E. and John Cole.

HEPTINSTALL—In loving memory of Pvte. W. E. Heptinstall, late of 15th Field Ambulance, who died Nov. 6th, 1918, in France, aged 28 years.

I miss you, God knows, and mourn you unseen,
And memories are sacred of days that have been;
But unknown to the world you stand by my side,
And whisper, "Dear sweetheart, death cannot divide."
—From his sorrowing Fiancée, Nellie.

MARKWICK—In loving memory of Pvte. Willie Markwick, K.O.Y.L.I., Pontefract, son of Mr. Henry Markwick, Northgate, Pontefract, killed in action in France, October 3rd, 1918.

For those left behind, the pain of loss would last for years.

and a multitude of hand flags gave a decidedly happy tone. But beneath the gaiety of the crowd there was the shadow of the absence of the departed, and it was to be noted as the procession passed that there were glistening eyes of mother, widow, sister, or sweetheart in window and doorway. It was, after all, a day of grief and remembrance for some.'

That afternoon, a procession of decorated lorries and horse-drawn wagons covered in red, white and blue bunting set out. The Knottingley boy scouts created a display on one showing a hospital scene with a wounded soldier lying in a tent and being cared for by nurses and orderlies. Behind them a second lorry carried Lily Starks dressed as Britannia and surrounded by soldiers and sailors. The paper reported that 'these tableaux evoked both favourable comment and applause'. With the Knottingley Prize Band in the lead the procession set off through crowded streets. Behind them came children on decorated bikes and tricycles and even one little boy leading a goat wearing the Union Jack, a group of local veterans dragging an effigy of the kaiser in a hand cart, and contingents from every school in the area, most of the girls in white, with 'wagons full of the tiny tots of the infants' schools, some singing the National Anthem, and practically all attempting to wave their flags over the edges of the wagons'.

When everyone had gathered on the Flatts, they were led in a rendition of *All People that on Earth do dwell* before a presentation was made to local hero Company Sergeant-Major Albert Penistone of the 6th York and Lancasters, who had won the Military Medal. Having served for four years in the Dardanelles and France, Albert was also entitled to wear the *Croix de Guerre* of France alongside his other medals, and an effusive Councillor Worfolk spoke of the courage and tenacity of the fighting men. CSM Penistone said he 'had done but his duty' but adding he promised that 'if ever there was another war he would do his best again'. After the cheering died away, the procession set off again to the Town Hall, where tea was served by their teachers to 1,760 children from local schools, and each was given a special commemorative mug. In contrast to the grim war years, there was plenty of food, 'more than some of the guests could eat at the time'.

That evening, a sports event was held in a field at Bank's Garth with

Standing 'sentinel on the road on which so many thousands of their soldiers took their first step on the way to their Great Adventure', Pontefract's war memorial today.

prizes of books, craftwork sets and scouts' equipment for the finalists who rushed to take part. Hilda Link won the under-10 60-yard skipping event and Alice Barker the under-10 egg-and-spoon race. Eleven-year-old Rotsey Spencer won the boys' sack race and Sam Stones the potato race. Even a shower at 9pm could not dampen spirits for long, though a longer rainfall later put paid to the dancing. All went home, tired but happy, carrying a special souvenir programme printed in red and blue.

The next day, a service of thanksgiving was held at the Town Hall, involving all ministers from every place of worship around town. Each had held a separate service before coming together for a united act of worship during which, it was reported, Baptist minister Reverend James Heselton spoke of: 'cause for rejoicing because the nation had a brighter outlook than ever before, because our neighbours were well disposed towards us; other countries were looking up to us; and because our children would receive a richer heritage in education and religion. Society had in the past been built on caste; in the future it would be built on ability; and in time it would be built on goodness … The dawn of peace was breaking, and we must look to a noon of unspeakable glory.'

It was a glorious dream but the reality was harsher. Within a week, 250,000 miners across the country were on strike. Unusually, the strike had spread to the men who operated safety precautions to maintain the pits and the *Chicago Tribune* of 24 July reported that seven pits were already flooded with a dozen more at serious risk if pumps were not started within forty-eight hours. The government response was to send in Royal Navy stokers to man the pumps and prevent flooding. Fearing reprisals, it also sent in armed troops to protect the sailors. They were not needed – even the most militant of the strikers knew that once a pit flooded it was lost and that attacking the sailors would mean the loss of their livelihoods, so relations were generally good.

It would set the pattern for the coming years. Britain had been almost bankrupted by fighting the war but its people had fought in the belief of a better future. That future, it was hoped, included a better deal for all – the problem was how to deliver it. In the cash-starved post-war economy it took almost five years for Pontefract to raise the £1,230 needed to erect a memorial for the 600 men and three women of the area known to have died in the service of their country. Castleford would not have a memorial until 1929. 'It was originally intended,' noted the *Pontefract Advertiser* on 23 September 1923, 'to inscribe the names of all the fallen on the memorial, but this idea had to be abandoned on two grounds – lack of space and lack of funds.' Almost 6,000 people turned out for the unveiling ceremony and heard General Ingham Brooke, one-time commandant of the barracks, address the crowd. The *Advertiser* reported that he told the waiting crowd that:

> [O]*n such occasions as that day's it was better that they should receive and take over these memorials in perfect silence. He agreed that it was well that they should keep silence, for silence was more appropriate than the most silvery oratory, but there were some things which he felt ought to be said, and which he wished to say. He asked the people of Pontefract to remember that the Memorial had been raised by public subscription to preserve the memory of the 600 men and three women or thereabouts, of the Borough, who served faithfully unto death; but he reminded them that the memorial did not close their debt to the dead or their dependants – for although on that occasion they offered their sympathy and respectful admiration to the bereaved ones – they must remember also the disabled who remained. There were the maimed, the halt and the blind also entitled to their sympathy and help. He wanted them to realise that the erection of that memorial was not, as it were, a receipt stamp placed at the end of the very long bill for the War. They still had the dependants and the disabled among them, and it should be their business to give them help and assistance and make their lives as happy as they could.*

It should not, he went on, be a memorial only to those who fell or to those who served in the two regiments whose badges adorned it, but its place in the town meant that anyone coming or going must pass it and in doing so remember what the war had meant to everyone.

In March 1924, 59-year-old Doctor Charles Carlton Moxon of South Milford was performing a post-mortem in his role as medical officer to the Joint Infectious Hospital Committee when he nicked his finger with a scalpel. Blood poisoning set in and he died soon after. It was an ironic end for a man who had given up his rank as surgeon-major to serve as a lieutenant in the South African war and who had subsequently led the 5th KOYLI throughout the First World War, surviving both without a scratch. Such were the vagaries of fate that men came unscathed through the worst fighting only to die in trivial accidents at home. In March 1923, 32-year-old rail guard Thomas Howard collapsed at the goods yard in Pontefract. He was taken to hospital where he was found to be suffering internal bleeding. A post mortem revealed a piece of shrapnel an inch long and three quarters of an inch thick had finally worked its way into his heart, years after he was hit in France.

Lt Col Charles Carlton Moxon, commander of 5th KOYLI throughout the war before returning to his career as a surgeon. After surviving the war unscathed, he died as the result of an accident with a scalpel during a post mortem in 1924.

Other deaths, though, were not accidental. In September 1924, a jury returned an open verdict on Frederick Jowsey, a Castleford slaughterman shot through the stomach by his own humane killer. According to his brother, Frederick 'had been a little depressed since he came home from the war'. Shortly afterwards, 49-year-old James Garnham of Pontefract asked for 'something to ease the pain inside so I can die quietly' after cutting his own throat. His family said he had been ill since his discharge from the army in 1919. Throughout the 1920s, the *Yorkshire Post* carried story after story about veterans committing suicide, the verdicts recording that the victim was 'affected by war service'. The war had cast a long shadow.

A century on, Hunt Street, once flag-bedecked home of Thomas Bryan, is just another anonymous row of terraced houses. Along Smawthorne Lane there are no reminders that at least seven men from this one street were killed or for the nineteen men from Tanshelf who never returned. Carleton Street is full of shoppers unaware of the riots that once took place. Few of the dog-walkers in Pontefract Park know of the bombs that fell here or of the Royal Flying Corps airfield they are walking on. Diners at a Chinese restaurant on Town End know nothing of Rhoda Walker or of the two wounded veterans who came into her shop in 1918.

The men, women and children who survived those tumultuous years are almost all gone. Soon, no child will ever again have chance to speak to someone who was alive when the events of this book took place but hopefully, from time to time, someone will look at Pontefract's stark memorial standing 'sentinel on the road on which so many thousands of their soldiers took their first step on the way to their Great Adventure' and pause. The homes those men lived in, the pubs they drank in, the shops they visited and the parks they played in are all still here. Away from the traffic and the hustle and bustle of modern life, somewhere at the edge of hearing, the voices of a lost generation can still be heard by those willing to listen.

Selected Bibliography

Bond, Lt Col R.C., *History of the King's Own Yorkshire Light Infantry in the Great War 1914-1918*, London: Percy Lund, Humphries & Co 1929

Johnson, M.K., *Saturday Soldiers*, Doncaster: Museum Service 2004

Magnus, L., *History of the West Riding Territorial Forces in the Great War*, London: Kegan Paul, Trench Truber 1921

Wyrral, E., *The History of the 62nd (West Riding) Division 1914–1919*, London: The Bodley Head Ltd

Newspapers

Doncaster Chronicle

Pontefract Advertiser

Pontefract and Castleford Express

Wakefield Express

Yorkshire Post

Yorkshire Evening Post

Index